The Ambitious Stylist

THE AMBITIOUS STYLIST

Making the Most of Cosmetology School

MARTHA LYNN KALE

THE AMBITIOUS STYLIST

Making the Most of Cosmetology School

FIRST EDITION

ISBN   978-1-5445-4641-4   *Hardcover*
       978-1-5445-4640-7   *Paperback*
       978-1-5445-4642-1   *Ebook*

For Trevor, Ford, and Luke. You are my "three great things."

For Mom, my biggest cheerleader!

CONTENTS

CONTENTS

INTRODUCTION

"I'M QUITTING MY JOB AND GOING TO COSMETOLOGY SCHOOL."

I said those same words to my roommate, my boss, and my mom. I expected all of them to try to talk me out of it. After all, who earns a college degree in advertising, lands a high-paying job in another state, and then quits to go back to school to learn to do hair?

Any one of those people could have laughed or even cried (looking at you, Mom!), but none of them did. Instead, they all responded with some version of, "Fun! How can I help?"

So, I moved out of my cute, single-girl apartment, sold my brand-new Tahoe, and moved back home. I went from wearing heels and making my own schedule to putting on a uniform and clocking in and out every Tuesday through Friday, 8:30 a.m. to 5:00 p.m.

My own hairstylist warned me cosmetology school would be challenging. She actually said I would hate it. But I'm an optimist. I figured it couldn't be *that* bad. It would be like art school: lots of creatives honing their craft to do what they love. I expected to spend my days chatting about current color trends. I expected to find camaraderie with fellow students who were all "in the trenches" together with the same goal.

Boy, was I wrong.

Cosmetology school was brutal. I wasn't prepared for the difficult book work (hello, *Skin Disorders and Sanitation*), or dealing with clients who wanted to pay five dollars for a haircut, or fellow students who were bored and unmotivated. I was definitely not prepared to have barely a half hour to grab the cheapest lunch I could find (my health tanked while I was in school). I was not prepared for standing on my feet seeing clients at school and then going straight to my retail job, where I stood on my feet for another four to five hours. I was not prepared for how lonely I felt because my fellow students didn't share my goal. I wanted to create an entirely different life for myself; many of them didn't seem to have any goals at all.

BRIDGING THE DISCONNECT

Sound familiar? Does the reality of your cosmetology school experience fall short of your expectations?

You are definitely not alone.

Not only can cosmetology school be challenging, it is sometimes ineffective. It doesn't always prepare students like you to enter the workforce, let alone land a dream job in a dream salon. There can be a big disconnect between the classroom time required to get the license and using the license to do hair.

In the past thirteen years as a salon owner, I have conducted over five hundred job interviews. No matter how many hours they logged, or where they went to school, or what their background was beforehand, most were not ready for the interview or the stylist position. They rarely had a proper résumé, dressed appropriately for the interview, or followed up with a simple thank-you email afterward. Most of the time, the person who showed up did not at all match the person I had seen online through social media. Bottom line: most of these cosmetology school grads were not ready to enter the workforce.

Isn't school supposed to set you up for success? In theory, yes, but that often doesn't happen. In Texas alone, only half of the students with the required number of hours actually pass the written portion of their boards. Of those who pass the written, 10 percent fail the practical. Of those who pass both sections and start doing hair, only 30 percent are still in the industry five years later.

Think about that. Approximately two out of every three students drop a ton of money on their education, spend nine to twelve months going to school, wear themselves out logging their hours, work part time to make ends meet—and then say, "Nah, I'm gonna do something else."

Why is that?

There are many reasons, but here are the most common:

- **They lose momentum.** Students start off excited and starry-eyed like I did, and then they get discouraged and bored. They start skipping class, which prolongs their time in school. They don't have a cheerleader or mentor to encourage them to keep going, so they eventually give up altogether.
- **They don't have a client list, and they don't know how to build one.** You can't run a business in this industry without clients. Period. Unfortunately, most schools don't teach this skill.
- **They don't make enough money.** The average hairstylist in America makes around $30,000 per year. That's near the poverty level in most states.
- **They think they are ready and skip an apprenticeship.** This can be tempting, but thinking you are ready to go for it straight out of school is risky. Later I'll share how I made this same mistake.
- **They try to go the independent route and get overwhelmed.** Cosmetology school doesn't teach the different business models. It doesn't explain that if stylists do independent booth rental, they will not actually take home 100 percent of the service price. Out of that they have to pay for shampoo, conditioner, styling products, rent, towels, capes, shears, curling irons, brushes, hair dryers—everything you use in your business—in addition to taking care of tasks such as washing their own towels, scheduling

their clients, finding new clients, and cleaning their space. For many, it's too much.

- **They pick the wrong salon when they apply for their first job.** All salons are not created equal. Some have a bright, cheery, easy-listening vibe, and some have a darker, cutting-edge rocker feel. Students don't learn to think about what they want in a salon or where they would feel most comfortable. Then they apply for the first stylist position they find and end up miserable.

I have good news: It doesn't have to be this way! You can still make your dream a reality. I can be the mentor to share the information you aren't gaining in school.

Now, I know that not all beauty schools are the same and not all teachers are the same, but as with everything else in life, there's the good and the not so good. This book can help you embrace the opportunity you have at school and make the most of it, no matter what your school experience is like.

Here's what you'll learn in the pages that follow:

- Action items to keep yourself motivated and engaged when school gets tough
- Prompts to help you dream about why you're in school, what kind of salon you want to work in, and what kind of stylist you want to be
- Tips for building important service industry soft skills, like being friendly, open, and conversational
- How to network and start building your clientele now
- How to use blowouts to build trust and win clients
- How to intentionally create a personal brand and professional online presence
- Tips for researching salons and finding the one in your area that's a perfect fit
- How to use informational interviews to learn more about the salons you find

- Tips for creating a résumé that fits this industry
- A step-by-step preparation timeline for your first job interview
- Tips for accepting a job offer and getting off to a great start in your new career

Along the way, I'll give you action items, checklists, and email templates. I'll share real-life stories (though the names have been changed) and advice from stylists who have been where you are. I'll also provide reality checks and journaling prompts so you can start thinking about where you are and where you want to be.

How do I know these tips and tricks work?

I taught myself the skills in this book, and I've coached hundreds of apprentices in my salon—many of whom have gone on to make six figures much faster than their peers. (Are you surprised to learn that making six figures as a stylist is even possible? It most definitely is—*if* that's what you want and you work hard to get there.) I know that if you take even the smallest steps in implementing these tips, you will be far ahead of the crowd.

One note: cosmetology school does include nails and skin care, in addition to hair. In this book, we'll focus on landing a dream job as a hairstylist, but you can apply the same tips and tricks to pursuing a career as a manicurist or esthetician.

GET A JOURNAL

If you don't have a journal, buy one. Use it to answer the prompts in this book and to record your thoughts and feelings as you go through school. Someday you'll want to look back on these challenging days to remember how far you've come. I saved my calendar from the year I was in cosmetology school because I wanted to remember how crazy it was.

MY PURPOSE

Back to the "I'm quitting my job" story: It should have been clear to me, and everyone else, that I was meant to be a stylist. At recess, I was the girl braiding my friends' hair instead of playing on the monkey bars. I was the one doing everyone's hair and makeup before high school formals and prom. In one of my favorite childhood pictures, I'm sitting on my mom's bed, brushing my hair.

But growing up in Alabama, *hairstylist* was not seen as a viable career opportunity. Most people I knew went to college and then business school, so that's what I did. I didn't ask myself, *Who am I? What's going to fill my cup? What kind of person do I want to be?* I simply followed the crowd. I enrolled at Auburn University and earned a business degree.

After graduation, I moved to Austin, Texas, for a job at one of the biggest advertising agencies in the country. The owner was all about purpose-based branding. He even wrote a book about it. He believed that when it's all said and done, if you—and your business—don't have purpose, then you're just like the next competitor. Nothing sets you apart. The importance of having purpose and creating impact was ingrained in me.

I excelled in my role, but I wasn't working in my purpose and I made no money. It was entry level, after all.

After about three years, I left the agency and took a sales role at one of the most iconic magazines in Texas. Here, I learned what it's like to have my entire paycheck based on my output. If I didn't produce, I didn't get paid. At all.

I responded well to the pressure, and I started making decent money, but I still felt like I was faking it. This wasn't my thing and these weren't my people, but I didn't know what my thing was, so I just kept going because that's what everyone else was doing.

Then one day my stepdad sat me down and said, "You know, I really think you should think about owning your own business."

His comment caught me by surprise. "What kind of business? I'm not gonna start an ad agency. I don't wanna start a magazine."

These were the things I was trained to do in some capacity, but none of them sounded appealing.

"Well, what would you do if money were no object? You do have to love what you're doing when you start a business because you will go through seasons where you don't get paid."

I didn't give him an answer that day, but the wheels started turning. *What do I love? What would I do even if I didn't get paid?*

Pretty quickly, the answer became clear: I love hair and makeup. I love helping people feel good about themselves. What career would allow me to do that? Being a stylist.

Soon after that conversation, I talked to my own hairstylist about my idea. "Is this crazy?" I asked.

"No, it's not crazy. But I'm warning you—cosmetology school won't be easy. You might even hate it. But you'll get through it and have an amazing career."

So I toured a few cosmetology schools and talked to some of the owners. One conversation in particular stood out. "Look out there on the floor," Wendi said. "There's probably two stylists out there who will ever make over a hundred thousand dollars."

I didn't say anything to Wendi, but in my mind I had accepted the challenge: I would be one of those two.

At that point, the decision to switch careers was made. I told my roommate, boss, and mom; I moved back home; and I started cosmetology school.

After graduation, I worked at three different salons in three years. I don't recommend this plan. In fact, I'll give you tips to avoid it!

Still, during that time I showed that I knew how to sell myself and my skills. Ten months out of school, I was a finalist for Best Hairstylist in Austin, and in 2010 I was named Best Hairstylist and runner-up for Best Colorist by a local magazine. In 2012, I won Best Highlights and was named a "Rising Star" in the fashion community of Austin.

After my first three years of bouncing around, I shifted from stylist to salon owner and Mirror Mirror was born. We were named best new salon in 2011 and grew from five to eleven to nineteen chairs in thirteen years.

Since then, we have been on the Inc. 5000 list of fastest growing privately held companies in America three times. We have been listed as a Top 200 Salon by *Salon Today* magazine for the past eight years.

These accomplishments didn't come without struggles. I've been in your shoes. I've done many things wrong. I want to help you avoid those mistakes.

YOUR PERSONAL CHEERLEADER

As a child, I attended a private school with kids primarily from two-parent homes and fathers who were doctors and lawyers. My mom was a single parent who worked extremely hard as a sales manager at a local radio station so I could have this expensive education.

At parents' night during first grade, we kids went around and announced what we wanted to be when we grew up. The most common answers were doctors, veterinarians, and dentists. When it was my turn, I stood up and said, "I want to be a professional cheerleader." I'm sure my mom wondered why she was spending all that money when her daughter wanted to be a cheerleader.

In middle school I took the first step toward my dream: I became a cheerleader, and in eighth grade I went to New York and performed in the Macy's Thanksgiving Day parade. Then I grew six inches between eighth and ninth grade, making me quite a bit taller than most collegiate cheerleaders. My professional cheerleading dream died.

But did it? As a salon owner and coach of new stylists, I cheer people on every day. In this book, I'll be cheering you on.

As you're reading this, you may be in school, bored out of your mind. You may be wondering what you've gotten yourself into. Cosmetology school may not be *at all* what you expected, and you may be on the verge of quitting.

Don't do it! You can have the career you dreamed of.

I'm going to help you remember why you enrolled in the first place. I'm going to give you the tools to live out your dream and not become a statistic. I won't give you technical how-to for coloring or cutting, but I will provide tips and tricks that will help you succeed no matter what school you attend, no matter what state you live in, no matter what kind of stylist you want to be, and no matter what kind of salon you want to work in.

The good news is that you've selected one of the most creative, rewarding, lucrative careers out there. You have the opportunity to make your passion your paycheck.

The bad news is that school stands between you and that career.

But that's okay. *The ambitious stylist takes ownership of her time in school.* By the end of this book, you will have an action plan to thrive right now in school and start planning for a fun and fulfilling career.

Yes, it will take some work. But you've already shown you're ambitious because you picked up this book. You can do this!

PART I

Dream and Learn

Chapter 1

START WITH THE END IN MIND

IMAGINE IT'S YOUR FIRST DAY AT YOUR NEW SALON. YOU WALK in to find an eclectic vibe, with vibrant fashion colors in the stylists' hair. The rock music is loud and the energy is high. The stylists chat with their clients as they cut the latest style. As you look around, a client walks past you with that "I paid good money for this, but I don't want you to know it" air. You can tell they're champions of diversity and inclusion here, and you feel right at home, knowing you will be able to thrive as the artist you are.

Or maybe you walk in to find a more masculine, sleek tone: barber shop meets New Age, a salon owned by a "celebrity stylist"—or someone who considers themselves one. The feel is industrial, decorated with reclaimed wood and an old bicycle hanging on the wall. Every stylist sports an ironic rocker tee, and there are hats and tats everywhere. The vibe oozes, "Honey, sit down. I can fix this." And they do, for the price of a monthly car payment, but the clients don't care because they eat up the status of getting their hair done there.

Or maybe you enter the blonde factory, decorated in soothing blush tones or boho chic, luxurious but still welcoming. A bubbly receptionist greets you up front and remembers your name. She leads you into a room of stylists who are *ready*—hair fresh, makeup fresh, dressed in the latest trends. They all look like influencers, selling confidence to their clients from the moment they walk in the door. Whether they want to "cut it all off!" or add length by way of extensions, these clients are well taken care of.

Or maybe you imagine a combination of all three and more. You smell the products, feel the comfortably worn upholstery in the waiting room, hear the familiar tunes, see the tasteful floral arrangements. And most importantly, you see yourself standing behind a chair, shears in hand, living your best life.

Which scenario hits home for you? Have you thought about the environment you'd like to work in, the clientele you'd like to serve, the product lines you'd like to sell? If not, this chapter is your invitation to dream, to figure out where you want to work and with whom.

If you're like most cosmetology school students, at some point during your training you will think, *What have I done? School is nothing like being in a salon!* To make it through this period, you have to figure out why you're there in the first place and what you want from your career when you're done. Then you have to keep your eye on the prize.

REMEMBER THE GOAL

One school administrator told me that her biggest challenge is keeping students focused on the basics: correct ergonomics, proper sanitary practices, and so on. The students follow celebrity stylists and influencers on TikTok, and they want to jump to the trendy cuts and coloring styles they see online.

Those things are exciting and possible—but you have to learn the basics first. You have to take the classes, log the hours, and pass the written test. If you can't pass the boards, you won't get your certification. You won't become a stylist. Period.

So, when class gets boring—and it will—remember the goal: to pass the test and get your certification. Then you can go out there and test out some of the advanced techniques you see online or become an influencer.

WHY ARE YOU HERE?

If you were to ask a roomful of stylists about their journey to cosmetology school, you would get a variety of answers. My guess is most did not go straight from high school to cosmetology school, partly because there's still a stigma around "doing hair" for a living. As I experienced, there's spoken and unspoken pressure to go to a "real" school, earn a "real" degree, and get a "real" job.

As a result, when many stylists start cosmetology school, they are extra excited because they are *finally* doing what they always wanted to do in the first place. And then the harsh reality hits and their excitement fades. During those moments, it's so important to remember why you enrolled in school.

I talked to several stylists I've worked with over the years, as well as some high-profile industry influencers (I included the influencers'

Insta handles in case you want to check them out), and asked them, "Why did you go to cosmetology school?"

Here are some of their responses:

"I went to college and after switching my major like four times my parents were like, 'What's the plan here?' I'm the oldest of four and they didn't have a ton to give but were trying to be fair to help all of us out as much as they could, and they could tell I was floundering.

"I didn't have a plan on what I was going to do or what I wanted to be (looking back, it seems normal at twenty to not know), so I took a semester off and was dating a girl at the time whose little sister was going to cosmetology school, and she would bring home mannequin heads and all that and I would mess around with them. She told me I should look into hair because it was creative and 'you could make a lot of money.'

"I told my parents and they were super supportive, and I went from there.

"I think my story is probably pretty standard. Lots of people don't really mesh with the scholastic thing, are more creative, and funnel into aesthetics. I definitely have no business being in this industry if we are basing things on how I grew up. I knew nothing about hair. My mom has had the same hairstyle (a little pixie) my whole life and took me and my brothers to military barber shops, neighbors who said they could cut us, or gave us a cheap pair of clippers and put us in the garage to take care of our own."

—GREG PIKE, SENIOR BALAYAGE SPECIALIST

"My initial push toward cosmetology was for the flexibility and creative nature. I didn't want to sit behind a desk anymore; it was suffocating. But by the time I graduated, the parts that fueled me became more about the client connection/relationships, the constant growing, learning, stretching but most of all being able to create something visually for someone that could inspire me while also empowering them."

—PAYTON KELLER, STYLIST

"I had gone to college and got a bachelor in sociology/criminal justice. In the meantime, throughout college and after, I was landscaping for about six years, trying to find a job in law enforcement. It was very discouraging.

"When I was about fifteen years old, my brother used to cut his friends' hair in our garage (he was pretty artsy). He showed me how to cut with clippers then I started gathering my friends in the garage to cut their hair as well. So I was cutting hair (just men's) throughout high school and college. So after the whole law enforcement thing didn't pan out, I was like, 'Ya know what, I think I wanna go to school to cut hair' because I enjoyed it. So I enrolled in Paul Mitchell."

—BRETT MELNICK, SENIOR STYLIST AND EDUCATOR

"I always loved doing hair, playing with my friends' hair, learning how to style. But I never thought of it as an option. I thought I had to go to school, which wasn't horrible. I dreamed of becoming a therapist—still my big dream. I ended up having to drop out due to panic attacks that were occurring almost every week.

"So I moved home and was working a dead-end job when a traumatic event led me to start therapy. My therapist advised me that finding a purpose and moving toward a purpose was the best next step.

"I mentioned my two loves—hair and therapy—and she told me to go to cosmetology school."

—BRANDY DRISKILL, STYLIST

"I was sitting around in my early twenties, kinda floundering. A stylist friend and I were having cocktails in his kitchen. After I told him a story about how much I loved playing with Barbies and my sister's friends' hair as a kid, he just looked at me and said, 'Get your ass into beauty school!'

"It never seemed like an option for me for some reason, but when he told me that, I instantly felt recharged and I toured a school the next week."

—BRETT WILSON, SENIOR COLOR SPECIALIST AND EDUCATOR

"I had two different career paths prior to going to cosmetology school. First I worked in HR, then realized how cutthroat it was and that often people don't like you when you are in HR. Then I decided I wanted to teach, so I went to school for my master's and taught for a few years in a juvenile detention center in a jail. Then COVID hit and things changed—like they did for so many. I wanted to do something that I wasn't going to hate and that wouldn't be so emotionally draining. So I reverted back to what was my artistic outlet. Even before school I cut and colored everyone in my family's hair, and surprisingly even my friends let me have a go at their hair. It was exploring an avenue of making a living with something I loved.

"After cosmetology school, my 'why' evolved, and I realized that hair is a huge part of people's identity. When you can tap into that and create something they love, it's both satisfying for me as an artist but it can also change someone's self-esteem. Knowing that hair is something you can't really hide—I think it's so important and more than 'we play with hair'—we can change the way someone looks at themselves. I may not be changing the world, but for a moment, I am changing their world for the better, and that's something I'll never get tired of doing."

—NATALY SYLVA, EXTENSION SPECIALIST

"My start began when I was around fourteen years old. A friend of mine and I shared in the purchase of a pair of clippers and started cutting each other's hair. By the time I was a senior in high school, I was cutting all my friends' hair in my garage. I never considered doing hair as a career, I just knew I loved it. After graduation, a friend of mine was a receptionist at a salon near my house. She was actually changing jobs and was helping them find her replacement. She called me because she knew I liked the industry. After meeting them, I just knew it was a good

fit. Three months later, I was enrolled in cosmetology school. That was almost twenty-eight years ago."

—CHRIS JONES, COFOUNDER, SALON BUGATTI (@CHRISJONES_HAIR)

"The reason for getting into cosmetology school was because my mom did hair. She also owned a salon, and I worked as her receptionist when I was sixteen after school. She then saw how I was with clients and people and encouraged me to go into doing hair."

—ANTHONY HOLGUIN, OWNER/CELEBRITY STYLIST,
AMAVIA ARTISTRY (@ANTHONYHOLGUIN)

"I got into cosmetology because I have always had an interest in all things beauty. When I was graduating high school, no other schools or programs resonated with me. Beauty school was the only thing I could really see myself doing."

—MELANIE HASSON, EDUCATOR/MASTER
COLORIST (@MELANIEMHASSON)

"I always knew from a very young age that hair was my calling. I gave all of my Barbies haircuts lol! I decided to go to a vocational high school so I could get my cosmetology license as soon as possible. The week after I turned eighteen, I got my license. I worked at a few different salons at first, trying to find the right fit. I assisted, answered the phones, cleaned, and was the coffee girl! I started from the ground up!"

—SARAH CABRAL, BALAYAGE SPECIALIST/EDUCATOR (@SARAHZSTYLZ)

"My Nana owned a hair salon in the small town I grew up in. In high school I always knew I wanted to go to cosmetology school. I loved to make people feel beautiful and confident. I always loved talking to people and knew I could utilize that in the beauty industry, so I decided to go to cosmetology school."

—STEPHANIE BROWN, HAIRSTYLIST (@VIVIDSANDBALAYAGE)

"I come from a family of beauty professionals. I was in the salon from the time I was a baby until now. I always knew I had a calling for the cosmetology field, and I fell in love with doing hair.

"I actually went to cosmetology school two times. First in 2014. I dropped out in 2015 because I let my anxiety get in the way of my dreams, and I let the opinions of other people dictate my life. I took a couple years off from school, worked on myself, and decided I was done letting anxiety control my life. I went back in 2017, graduated in 2018, and haven't looked back since."

—TAYLOR DELLATORRE, HAIRSTYLIST/EDUCATOR,
OWNER, SAGE SALON (@TAYLORDIDMYHAIR)

Do any of these stories sound familiar? Or is your "why" completely different? Maybe you:

- love people and want to take care of them every day
- have a servant's heart and hospitality is at your core
- are looking for a flexible schedule
- are an artist at heart and want to create something new every day
- didn't want to go college or a different trade school, so you ended up here
- were the kid braiding everyone's hair at recess
- want to continue the family tradition: your mom and grandma were both stylists; now it's your turn
- want to make your own hours so you can spend time with your kids after school

Or maybe your reason is a combination from this list, or something completely different. There is no right or wrong answer!

Journal Challenge

Why did you go to cosmetology school?

After you figure out your "why," write it down. Be able to articulate exactly why you are in school. The more specific, the better, and the sooner into your school journey that you articulate it, the better. You will be able to go back and look at your "why" on the days when school is boring and hard and unmotivating. Years down the road, you will be able to remember where you started. I really wish someone had given me this advice. I would love to be able to go back and read my original "why."

So, put down the book, pick up your journal, and write it down.

Here's an added challenge: share your "why" with someone—a classmate, your sister, your bestie. Share it at theambitiousstylist.com. Putting it out into the world makes it real.

If you're feeling alone or like your "why" isn't valid, talk to your classmates. Ask them why they're in cosmetology school. You might be surprised to learn you're not the only one who wants to help people or loves the therapy aspect.

WHAT DO YOU WANT?

Now that you've figured out why you're in school, it's time to dream. What kind of stylist do you want to be? Where do you want to work?

I recommend starting with you, the stylist. If you begin with the salon, you might start bending yourself to fit into an environment that isn't really you. It's better to know yourself and what kind of stylist you want to be, and then find a salon that fits.

WHAT KIND OF STYLIST?

When you're thinking about what kind of stylist you want to be, start with the kind of clients you want to have. Then work backward: how can you become the kind of stylist they come to?

Remember: this is a people business. You're working with people all day long. So, who do you want to spend your time with? Who is your dream clientele? Is it moms? The college crew? Corporate professionals? Edgy hipsters?

Identifying your dream clientele has a lot to do with common lifestyles. If you're a mom, your ideal clients may be other moms who have a similar afternoon schedule that involves picking up kids from school and then going home. If you're fresh out of school, your ideal client may be close to your age—the college age or sorority girl crowd. On the other hand, if you like to stay up late and start work late, your ideal clients won't be the corporate crew who want a 7:00 a.m. appointment.

Your clientele has a big impact on the direction you take as a stylist. If you want to serve the hipster crowd, for example, you better hone your hair-cutting skills because you'll be doing a lot of trendy cuts. If you want to serve a more mainstream crowd, plan on focusing on classic services and silhouettes. If you want to cater to a more high-maintenance crowd, get certified in extensions and practice your highlighting skills. Knowing your dream clientele gives you direction in school. Think through their lens: what kind of stylist would they want to go to?

I tend to go to a stylist with similar interests, someone who is at a similar stage in life. I'm going to sit in her chair for a few hours. I want our conversation to be easy and organic. Would someone who is completely different from me do a perfect job on my hair? Maybe. But skills being equal, I'm going to pick the person I naturally get along with.

So, how can you become likable to your ideal client? Becoming likable to the people you want to serve should not be hard. It should not involve pretending or putting on a mask. Faking it is exhausting, and at some point that mask is going to fall off.

As we'll discuss later, one of the most important parts of landing your dream job working with your dream clients is being your true, authentic self at all times—in person and online. We'll get to personal brand in Chapter 5. For now, just focus on being your fabulous self, and you'll be likable to your ideal clients.

THINK OUTSIDE THE SALON

Wedding work is a great way to build your business as a new stylist. Often there is no coloring or cutting involved. You're just doing updos, curls, and special occasion styling. Consider adding this to your skillset while you're still in school and getting your feet wet.

I did a ton of weddings when I was in school and starting out. Not only was the money good but it also exposed me to people beyond the bride—bridesmaids, moms, mothers-in-law, cousins, friends—who later booked appointments. You also end up with beautiful photos for your portfolio.

Don't know how to get started with weddings? Enlist some local wedding planners. Once you prove yourself with one or two, you will often end up on their preferred vendor list, and the rest is history!

In addition to identifying your dream clientele, you have to figure out what you want to do as a stylist. Do you want to do photo shoots and set work for magazines or websites? Do you want to specialize in weddings? Do you want to work off-site, traveling to someone's house to do highlights in their fancy bedroom? Or do you want to work on-site, in your own salon, behind your own chair?

Also think about your specialty: is it cutting or coloring or extensions, or do you want to do it all? If you're not sure, don't panic. You have time in school to figure it out. It's like picking a major in college: you might start off "undeclared" and then figure out what you really love.

As you learn how to do these different services, pay attention to your likes and dislikes, to what comes easy and what is simply not your thing. Picture yourself doing extensions or highlights day after day, year after year. Does that thought excite you, terrify you, or bore you to tears? How about coloring or trendy cuts? Pay attention to your gut reaction and let it guide you.

Journal Challenge

What kind of clients do you want to work with?

What service do you want to be known for?

WHAT KIND OF SALON?

You may choose to focus on weddings or photo shoots, but at some point in your career, especially right out of school, you're likely to work in a salon. So, what kind of salon do you want to work in? At the beginning of the chapter, we painted the picture of three salon environments. Yes, they were stereotypical and a bit exaggerated, but still—did any of those appeal to you?

When you think about your dream salon, consider everything from size to commuting distance to decor to music. For example:

- Do you want something close to home, or do you care more about working in the environment where your clients live?
- Do you like it loud and bright, or do you prefer a quiet, softly lit spa-like atmosphere?
- Do you want to work with young clients and stylists, or does age make no difference?

- Do you want to start early and leave early, or are you a night owl?
- Do you prefer fluffy and feminine, or sleek and masculine?
- Do you prefer a more boutique-size environment, or do you thrive around lots of people?

Maybe you've never considered any of these questions. That's okay! Take out your journal and start now. You could save yourself—and any salon that hires you as an apprentice—a lot of headaches if you know what you want from the beginning. You won't have to quit and start from the beginning at another salon.

Journal Challenge

Look at the bullet list of questions in this section and write down your answers. Let yourself dream in vivid detail: sights, sounds, smells.

I hope it's clear that there are no right or wrong answers to these questions. You simply need to figure out what you want. And it's better to do that up front. If you know that you have an unreliable car and hate commuting, then find a salon close to home. If your boyfriend is in a band and you watch him play three nights a week, then find a salon that allows you to come in at ten in the morning.

The key is to know yourself. Be honest about your likes and dislikes. Then figure out how to create your dream job.

DREAM BIG

Imagine it's five years from now and you've become a stylist. How would someone describe you? Where do you live? Where do you work? What kind of car do you drive? Where do you go on vacation?

Start thinking about those things now. The end goal of cosmetology school is to use your passion to create a paycheck, and then use that paycheck to create the life you want. You're not putting yourself through misery to make minimum wage, are you?

Dream in detail: the more specific your vision, the more likely you are to get it. Then write it down. Psychology professor Gail Matthews found you are 42 percent more likely to reach your goals if you write them down, and your hairstylist dreams are no different. Tell a friend. Share your "why" at theambitiousstylist.com, and while you're there, read the "why"s of fellow cosmetology school students and stylists. You will find accountability, as well as encouragement, in sharing your dreams with others.

As we've said, there's good news and bad news around the path you've chosen: The good news is that you have picked an amazing career. You can have what you dream for yourself and your salon. The bad news is you have to get through school to get there. *The ambitious stylist accepts the bad but focuses on the good.*

In the next chapter we'll talk about the study skills you'll need to pass the test and get your certification, as well as some practical skills you can learn during your classroom hours.

BAD HAIR DAYS

Remember: you will have bad days in cosmetology school—and in life. Even bad weeks. I promise.

What can you do to keep yourself going?

- Reread your "why."
- Take a bath.
- Go out to dinner with a friend.
- Go for a hike/walk.
- Cook a nice meal.
- Read a novel.
- Go to a movie.
- Volunteer your time.
- Do something artistic that isn't hair related.

Do yourself a favor and make a list now of things to do when you're having a bad day. Add it to your journal. Then when you find yourself tempted to skip class or even quit, check your list and pick the one that sounds the most rejuvenating.

Chapter 2

CLASSROOM TIME

TRIVIA TIME! WHAT PERCENTAGES OF TEXAS COSMETOLOGY STU-
dents passed the written exam in 2023?

Believe it or not, only *50 percent* passed the written exam. Half!

Now consider this: to move on to the practical portion of the test, you have to pass the written. If you don't pass, you're out. That means in 2023 alone, nearly nineteen thousand students spent an average of $18,500 each and couldn't even take the second part of the test, let alone get their certification.

I'm here to help you be in the 50 percent that passes, and I'm really hoping that percentage goes way up! It won't be easy. You'll have to study. But you can do it.

For now, set aside the dreams from the last chapter. We started with dreaming because you'll need to keep your eyes on that prize in the coming months. Right now it's time to come back to reality: You are in school. It's time to learn. You have to pass.

In this chapter, we'll talk about the study skills you'll need to pass the exam, as well as the soft skills you can start practicing during your time in school.

UNDERLYING ASSUMPTIONS

Before we get to the skills, I want to share a couple of assumptions I'm making about you because you picked up this book. Don't worry, they're all good.

YOU'RE AMBITIOUS

First, I'm assuming you're ambitious. You want to succeed. You want to become an excellent stylist with a thriving business. And most importantly, you're willing to work hard to get there.

Ambitious students take responsibility for their own success. They see the goal, and they do what it takes to get there. If you feel like you're not being prepared in school, don't blame the teachers or the school. The state board doesn't care where you studied or what teachers you had. They only care if you can pass the exam.

So, figure out what you need to know. If you're not getting that information, figure out how to get what you need. You have the internet. Take ownership of your education.

Also, know the rules in your state. Can you retake the written portion if you fail the first time? If so, how many times can you retake it? Do you have to pass within a certain number of months from completing your school hours?

Again, you have the internet. If you can't find the exact information online, you can probably find a phone number for the state's Department of Licensing and Education.

Here's another hard truth: You will like some parts of cosmetology school more than others. You are required to learn skin and nails, in addition to hair. If you just want to do hair, then the skin and nails sections are going to be less interesting, maybe even painfully boring. Who wants to learn about sanitation and nail fungus, right?

So, what are you going to do? Complain? Scroll through Instagram? Do mannequin-head bowling (yes, that's a real thing)? Stop going to class? Or are you going to make good use of your time?

The following chapters will give you plenty to work on during these uninspiring days. When you're ambitious, you don't need to be micromanaged. You come up with ways to prepare for your future career right now!

If you hit a roadblock somewhere along the way, don't quit. Find another way around. Remember that picture you dreamed up in Chapter 1? (Oh, you didn't write it down? It's not too late!) Figure out how to get that dream.

YOU'RE A PEOPLE PERSON

Second, I'm assuming you're a people person. You can be introverted or shy, but at your core, you have to like people. If you don't, abort mission. Get your money back and get out now.

I didn't realize that I'm an introvert until I became a stylist. At the end of a long day cutting and coloring hair and interacting with clients, I would get into my car and sit in silence. I was completely drained because I had left it all on the floor. I loved taking care of people, but I needed to recharge afterward. That's okay. That's completely different from not liking people.

If you're introverted like me, you'll need to find ways to recharge. Go to a spin class, do a paint by number, walk your dog—find an activity you can enjoy without talking to people for a little while.

Whether you're introverted or extroverted, your focus is the same when you're on the floor: it's all about the client. If you had a bad morning, don't bring that negative energy to the salon. Put a smile on. Take care of your client. If you don't like your new client's outfit or her favorite sports team or political views, keep it to yourself. Leave your judgmental attitude at the door. Take care of your client.

As a stylist, you are touching another person's head and hair. That's an intimate action. Do everything you can to help her relax and enjoy the experience. Learn how to steer the conversation; specifically, steer it away from politics, religion, and other hot-button topics. Keep it light and breezy.

I did hair through several election cycles when conversations could easily get heated. I knew I was doing my job when every single client thought I agreed with them and their candidate choice. I let them talk and nodded along, but I didn't contribute to the discussion one way or another. I listened and looked for a way to change the subject to something less touchy.

Depending on where you live, even college football can be a no-fly zone. You don't need to jump in with your favorite team or opinion about the client's favorite team. Let the comments roll off your back. Learn to see the other person's point of view no matter what you're talking about.

Even if you and your client happen to agree on every last thing, the person sitting in the next chair may not. Don't ruin her experience. You can talk about the loaded subjects at lunch or over drinks, but in the salon, keep it light and breezy.

KEY SKILLS

Being ambitious and loving people is a great place to start, but to realize your dream, you need a certification. And to get your certification, you have to pass the practical and written parts of the exam, which means you need solid study skills and technical skills. This book won't focus on technical skills, but you need them. You have to be good at what you do.

You also need certain soft skills to become a successful stylist, and the classroom is the perfect place to practice them.

STUDY SKILLS

Think back to the last time you were in school. How did you study? Did you use flash cards? How were your test-taking skills? Were you a last-minute crammer? How did that work out?

Better yet, think back to the class you hated most. How did you get through it? Did you need a tutor? Did you rewrite your notes?

Did you study with a buddy and talk through the content? Your experience preparing for the state board written section will most likely resemble preparing for tests in your most-hated classes.

Here's the good news: the test is multiple choice. And the bad news: multiple choice isn't going to help if you read a sanitation question and all four answer options look like they're written in a foreign language.

You need to give yourself a fighting chance. You need to figure out how to study and learn the material, even for those uninspiring sections.

Part of figuring out how to study is understanding what kind of learner you are. In other words, what is the best way for you to take in and retain information? If you're not sure, look online for a quiz to figure it out.

Here are the four types of learners along with an example of what might help each type remember information:

- **Visual learners** learn through seeing. They find it helpful to use highlighters, underlining, and colored font to break up their notes and make key points stand out.
- **Auditory learners** learn through listening. They find it helpful to read material out loud or listen to a recorded lecture. Discussing lessons with other people also helps since it allows them to hear content in a different way.
- **Read/write learners** learn through the act of writing. They find it helpful to make note cards and rewrite their notes.
- **Kinesthetic learners** learn through doing. They find it helpful to sit where they can actively participate in the lecture by asking or answering questions. Making models, drawing pictures, and using practice tests are also useful.

Journal Challenge

What type of learner are you? Do you learn better when someone gives you verbal instructions, or when you read the directions? If you need to remember a list of items, do you remember them best if you write them down, or repeat them as you count them off on your fingers?

If you're not sure, do a Google search for "What type of learner are you?" You should get a list of websites with quizzes to help you figure it out. Write down your answers in your journal. Then search for tips for studying as this kind of learner.

Don't try to fight the way your brain works. If you need to highlight or underline key ideas, do it. If you need to draw pictures or listen to a recorded lecture or rewrite your notes, do it. Figure out how you learn, what helps you retain info, and then take action.

The most important thing is to study throughout your time at school. Many schools pile on the book work early. The problem is, you can forget a lot of it as you move on and start working on your practical skills. When you find yourself bored in class, use the time to organize and review your notes. Then set aside time each week to review until you graduate. Put it in your calendar.

If you had test anxiety in high school and college, be ready for that to happen again. It's okay to feel nervous. Just don't let it keep you from moving forward. One intern was so scared to take the written portion that she kept putting it off. This dragged on and on. Finally, I laid down the law: "By tomorrow I need you to schedule your test. And I need you to think about whether you really want this."

Twenty-four hours went by, and I hadn't heard back from her. Now, if my prospective boss told me to do something in the next twenty-four hours, I would have done it immediately. She didn't. Needless to say, she also didn't get hired.

The same goes for the practical side. You will probably get nervous about people watching you and grading you as you cut and color hair. That's okay. Through practice, you can be ready for people to see and judge your work.

Pull up your big-girl pants. You're going to be tested in writing and in practice. You know what you struggled with in the past. You need to figure out how to get through it. *The ambitious stylist can do hard things.*

And remember: once you pass, you will *never* have to do this again—as long as you stay current on your continuing education.

SOFT SKILLS

Okay, you should be convinced that you need to brush up on those study skills. But don't stop there! You need study skills to pass the test, but you'll need other skills to succeed once you have your own chair. And the classroom is the perfect place to practice them.

People Skills

Remember our second assumption: you're a people person. Even if that's true, you can benefit from practicing your people skills. This is especially true if you're naturally shy.

There you are in a classroom of people from different backgrounds and with different reasons for attending cosmetology school. What a perfect time to get comfortable talking to strangers! Get in the habit of asking your classmates questions like, "Where are you from?" "What made you decide to go to cosmetology school?" "What shows are you streaming on Netflix?"

You may look around the room and think you have nothing in common with your classmates. Worse, you may start judging them—their hair, their clothes, their makeup or lack thereof. Stop yourself. Having a buddy can really help, and you never know who will turn out to be that person. Be open-minded, not judgmental.

Don't sit in the corner texting or scrolling. Get to know your classmates. As you talk, you'll most likely learn that you don't root for the same football team or hold the same political beliefs. That's a perfect opportunity to practice steering the conversation into safer, less controversial topics.

Stop Comparing

When you start doing mannequin work, don't look around and compare yourself to your classmates. Don't worry about how quickly your friend can roll a perm or highlight a head. People learn different skills at different paces. You might be slower to pick up foiling techniques, but quicker at blowouts. Run your own race. It's not a group project. It doesn't matter what they do or don't do. All that matters is what you do, so focus on perfecting your own skills.

As part of your training, at some point you will all do a version of a long, layered haircut and then blow it dry. You will do the same with a pixie cut and a bob. In each case, every single mannequin head will look different in the end, even though you're all performing the same service. The same would be true if you were all working on real people in a salon instead of mannequins in the classroom. Each stylist will execute the skills differently. Stop comparing yourself.

Don't compare yourself to social media either. Maybe you follow a stylist who has a hundred thousand followers. One of their posts shows a fancy new trick. You try it, but the result is not even close. You wonder, *Well, why can't I do that?* Because you're brand-new and they've been doing this for years. Repetition is your friend. Your first haircut will look very different from your hundredth. Focus on getting that repetition and practice, not what others are doing. Stop comparing yourself.

The same is true in the real world. I recently had a conversation with Erin, a stylist who is absolutely crushing her goals and is on track to be an extension specialist in our salon—a very coveted title. She was still struggling with comparing herself to the other extension artists in the salon, how they have more extension clients and post on social media more and so on. When I showed Erin the data (I love numbers because they aren't emotional), she saw that she was one of the top artists in the salon in terms of extension installs—a requirement to be a specialist. I also pointed out that the other girls were probably comparing themselves to her and thinking she was the one who had more clients.

Stay in your lane and focus on being the best you, and the rest will fall into place!

Be Open

To learn the tricks that work best for you, you have to be open to feedback and suggestions. For example, if your teacher suggests that you hold the brush a certain way, don't get defensive. Try it. You might find it works better for you. And if you don't, you can hold the brush the way you want when you're on your own.

You might go into school with a certain idea about the kind of artist you're going to be—maybe one who is known for doing blue and lavender hair. Then you go through your hours and start trying to build a clientele and realize, *Huh, I don't know many people who want blue and lavender hair.*

Or maybe you heard somewhere that to make money, you have

to do extensions. Then you start learning extensions in school and realize it's definitely not your thing. Now what? Don't force yourself to do a service you don't enjoy, just for the sake of money. Clients will sniff that out. Instead, shift gears a little and focus on another area you like. No big deal.

The whole cosmetology school experience will be mind-blowing. You'll learn you're not so interested in things you thought would be your jam. You'll discover hidden talents. You'll come out tougher because you faced challenges. Be open. You may think learning certain skills, like setting perms, is a complete waste of time, only to find they are all the rage among high school boys. Never say never.

In this industry, it all comes down to being good at your art and taking care of your people. If you can do those right, you'll be successful. You don't have to be on the same path as your neighbor, or stay on the same path throughout your career. There are many ways to be successful. The only way to find out which path is right for you is to experiment. And the best time to do that is right now, in the classroom, with mannequins and clients who are only paying ten dollars for a service. This is the safe zone.

LEARN TO MULTITASK

One of the beauties of working with mannequins is that they don't talk. That means you can really focus on your skills and not worry about carrying on a conversation at the same time.

However, in the salon, you need to be able to work with your hands and carry a conversation simultaneously. If you pause every time you speak, the service will take too long.

So, whenever you have live people in your chair, practice cutting and talking at the same time.

Dress the Part

It's easy to be lazy about your appearance when you're in school. No one's going to see you, right?

Maybe, but the day you wear holey sweats and a baseball cap might also be the day someone from your dream salon shows up to speak. Awkward.

View school as a dress rehearsal for your job. You don't need to show up wearing heels and a full face of makeup, but you should look put together. That doesn't mean spend a lot of money on a whole new wardrobe. Figure out your look, buy five versions of it, and you're set for the week. Your clients won't know what you wore yesterday. Plus, you'll likely be putting an apron over it anyway.

Some schools have a dress code, such as all black. You can still look sloppy in all black if your black shirt is faded or you're wearing black sweatpants or your black tennis shoes have a hole in them. Start practicing for your salon job now and put some effort into your appearance.

Also make sure your hair is clean and styled. Your hair is your best calling card, so get in the habit of doing it every day—even when you're only going to class. That doesn't mean wash/dry/curl every single day. Even a low ponytail can look chic if done well, and it takes five minutes. Would you go to a dentist with bad teeth? They might be skilled, but their calling card says otherwise. The same is true for you.

If you have a tendency to go too long between manicures and you have chipped nails, take that polish off until you can get back to the manicurist. No one wants to see chipped nails and color-stained fingers when the stylist is foiling their hair, fingers in their face. Even in the classroom.

Actually, people don't want dirty anything—fingernails, hair, clothes. No matter what style you're going for, you have to look like you bathe. If you look dirty, people may wonder if you sanitize your brushes and other tools.

Practice taking pride in yourself and your workspace. Wear

deodorant. Use breath mints. People don't want to smell you for two and half hours. If you're like Matthew McConaughey and phasing out deodorant, maybe reconsider. Neither the classroom or the salon is the venue for that experiment.

Your days in the classroom will be long and hard. You don't need to overdo it on your hair and makeup, but look intentionally put together. Plus, you'll feel better.

SAFE ZONE

Just in case you missed it: school will be boring sometimes. You will not be interested in every topic. Some sections will be more challenging than others. Sounds like life, right?

The answer is not to start skipping class. That creates bad habits for the future when you need discipline and focus to rise quickly. It also prolongs the torture now because you still need to log hours before you can take the exam and receive your license.

Instead, figure out what you need to do to remember the material and pass the test. Would it help to have a study buddy? Do you retain information better if you highlight your notes or rewrite them? Understand your learning style and then use it. Even if nail fungus and safety are uninspiring, you need to remember what you hear. The test is not a pick-and-choose buffet. You will be tested on all of it.

Also remember that the classroom time is the safe zone. You're working on mannequins, learning techniques, and practicing services. It's the perfect time to work on all kinds of soft skills you'll need on the floor. Don't sit in the corner on your phone. Get out there and practice.

Many students are ambitious and motivated when they start the program, and then find themselves in a slump when they get about a third of the way through. In Part II, we'll talk about how you can avoid this slump by focusing on one of the most important parts of your business: building a clientele.

Journal Challenge

When I was growing up, my mom had us tell her "three great things" at the end of every day. Her goal was to help us learn gratitude as a way of shifting our outlook on life. I do the same with my husband and children now.

This exercise is especially helpful when you're having a bad day. It will force you to think of the good things that have happened in the midst of the bad. It will teach you to be grateful.

Take out your journal. Write down three great things. Make this an everyday practice, because as I've said, you're going to have bad days.

PART II

Build a Clientele

Chapter 3

NETWORKING

HAVE YOU HEARD OF THE PARETO PRINCIPLE? THE NAME COMES from an Italian economist named Vilfredo Pareto who studied wealth distribution in Italy. He observed that 80 percent of the land was owned by 20 percent of the population. After looking at different parts of society, he suggested that this ratio could be found in many places: in farming, business, and more.

The general idea of the Pareto principle is that 80 percent of outcomes come from 20 percent of causes. For example:

- 80 percent of a company's sales come from 20 percent of its customers.
- 80 percent of a store's profits come from 20 percent of its brands.
- 80 percent of the errors in software come from 20 percent of the code.
- 80 percent of someone's productive work comes from 20 percent of their activities.

As a stylist, this means that 80 percent of your business will probably come from 20 percent of your clients.

If that's true, it makes sense to have a strong 20 percent, right? And the best way to do that is through *networking*.

In this chapter, we'll discuss tips you can use now to expand your circle and start building that 20 percent. Even if you are shy or new to your city, you can build a strong clientele through networking.

WHAT IS NETWORKING?

To be a successful hairdresser, you'll need a lot of clients who are willing to pay good money for your services—and by *a lot*, I mean three hundred, give or take, depending on the services you provide.

Don't worry. No one has three hundred clients when they start. They may not even have one. It's possible that a salon will give you three hundred clients when you get hired, but it's highly unlikely. So, you have to find them yourself. That's where networking comes in.

When you hear the word *networking*, you may think of stiff, formal corporate events. Chances are you opted into the salon industry because you wanted nothing to do with the corporate world where people wearing name tags on their button-down shirts stand around shaking hands and exchanging business cards. No, thank you!

VOICES FROM THE FIELD

Carolyn Holden has been in the industry for twenty years, and she is currently our Lead Stylist and Educator at Mirror Mirror. Here's what she had to say about networking:

The thought of "networking" can be intimidating when you are starting your career. Networking may sound cold or impersonal, possibly even disingenuous. However, it is quite the opposite. Networking requires two things: accessing the contacts you already have and accessing the contacts you *want* to have.

I started in this industry when I was twenty-one years old. I was building a clientele in my hometown, which did afford me certain advantages—I knew people! But, all of those people already had a hairstylist, so I still had to network and stick my neck out there! I started by sending a letter and a business card to every single person that would even recognize my name. This allowed me to reach the people I already knew and let them know what I was up to professionally. That initial contact paid dividends. Many of them gave me an opportunity to see them in my chair, and some kept the information for later use when they were searching for a new stylist and/or passed my information along to others.

I couldn't merely rely on contacts I already had. My goals necessitated that I reach beyond that. I got involved in local/social events and fundraisers. Think Fashion Week, bridal shows, sorority events, and fundraising opportunities to style hair for their event or donate a haircut or blowout. I also got involved in organizations that mattered to me personally: Junior League, my church, intramural social sports club, and book club/supper club with friends new and old.

These ways of networking don't sound cold or disingenuous, do they? No, I used contacts I already had and reached them personally to let them know what I was up to professionally—and then got involved locally with organizations that were near and dear to me and had fun along the way making new friends.

I do understand that we don't necessarily send letters and business cards anymore. Maybe we should?! Is that the personal touch that sets you apart? We all use technology to our advantage and think of ways to make it personal. Maybe a digital business card that you can exchange? Or follow up personally to everyone that "likes" or comments on your post.

Let's remember: networking is truly just the exchange of information and developing professional relationships. Make it personal and *you* and fun!

Networking in this industry is all about being genuinely interested in others. It's about expanding who you know and looking for ways to support and care for those people. It's about making deposits into those relationships more than taking withdrawals from them. It is much more than meeting people so you can ask for their business.

Remember what we said in Chapter 2: you have to be a people person. Working in a hair salon is literally and figuratively a hands-on people business. It's not a virtual role or a work-from-home environment. That means your best bet for building a strong clientele is in-person, face-to-face interactions—not phone calls or texts or emails or Instagram messages.

You have to be intentional. You have to get off your phone, go out in public, and meet real, live people. Don't think you have time for that? Check the screen time on your phone. I bet you spend hours each week—each day!—scrolling social media.

Don't get me wrong—social media can serve a purpose in meeting and interacting with people. It can definitely help you build your business. You can use social media to speak to those who already follow you, and some may eventually become clients.

But there's a whole world of people out there who are potential clients. People who live in your town who are bored with their hair or have been going to the same stylist for years just because it's easy. These people need you, and you have to find them.

Every social event is a possible networking event. Your friend's birthday party. Your boyfriend's work event. Your kid's school activity. Your part-time job outside of school.

I know—school is exhausting, and you may be working another job on the side. No matter how tired you are, you need to get out there. This is the best way to expand your circle and meet those people who might become your 20 percent.

LIST OF TWENTY

Three hundred clients sounds overwhelming, right? Let's start with twenty.

Take out your journal and write down twenty clients you don't have that you wish you did. Twenty people you know who could become clients if you simply asked them. Did you write them down? Go ahead. I'll wait.

Your List of Twenty will probably include close friends and family. Think about each of those people. What will it take to get them into your chair? Could you entice them with a free blowout? Do they love seeing pics of themselves on social media? Would they be up for modeling their fantastic hair on Instagram?

Come up with the perfect incentive for each person on your List of Twenty and then ask. Here are some invitations you can use for different scenarios. One note: Be specific. Give a precise date and time when you invite someone to come in.

- **Free blowout:** "Hey, I have a little time on X date at X time. Want to pop by for a blowout? My treat."
- **Free women's haircut:** "Huge favor. I have to show my teacher a simple haircut from start to finish. Just a trim, nothing dramatic. You have gorgeous hair, and you would make me look good! I have an opening on X date at X time. Would you be up for that?"
- **Free men's haircut:** "Huge favor. I have to show my teacher a men's cut from start to finish. Your hair is exactly what I need. Nothing crazy. I'll just clean it up. How far off are you from your next trim? I'd love to get you in by the end of the month."
- **Free highlight:** "Okay, you have the best hair. I have a little free time on X date at X time. Would you want to come play hair? We could even pop in a few foils and you'll get a bomb blowout and curls."

Make your invitations breezy and genuine. Speak the way you naturally speak. If you text your invitations, add an emoji or two if that's your style.

What if they say no? Who cares! Don't go silent if they say no; that's even more awkward. Simply say something like, "I totally get it. Can you think of anyone else who might be interested? I'd love to extend the same offer. Any friend of yours is a friend of mine."

Asking for referrals is a keyway to expand your circle, so the person who says no has just given you an opportunity to practice.

KEEP TRACK

Another important part of networking is keeping track of who you talk to, how they respond, what service you provide, and so on.

You already wrote down your List of Twenty. Now add some notes, for example:

1. Susan Smith, cousin. Messaged on 10/5. Came in on 10/15. Free blowout.
2. Jack Jones, friend. Messaged on 10/5. Said no, but referred me to Braden.

You'll start to see how quickly you reach out to your List of Twenty and beyond. Soon, you'll be at your next twenty.

21. Braden, Jack's friend. Messaged 10/9. Came in on 10/20. Free trim.

And then just keep going. How do you eat an elephant? One bite at a time. The same is true of building a clientele. Three hundred is overwhelming, but if you focus on building and expanding your List of Twenty one at a time, you'll build a solid clientele in no time.

If you ever get discouraged, look back at your list. You may be surprised to see that you already invited fifty people. Encourage yourself. That's huge progress!

You might also see patterns. Maybe the first ten people said no. Look at how you worded your invitation. Can you tweak something when you try with the next person?

No matter what, don't give up. If you only have five solid clients by the time you graduate, you'll be far ahead of most students.

As people on your List of Twenty say yes, move them to your list of clients. Then replace them with new potential clients. This way you're always working on a List of Twenty of clients you don't have that you should.

Before you are tempted to say, "I can't find *any* clients!" or "I'm new in town and I don't know *anyone*!" or "I can't think of *anyone* to ask!" let me give you a whole list of people you can reach out to:

- Extended family
- Acquaintances from high school or college
- Coworkers and/or bosses
- Sorority sisters or fraternity brothers
- Babysitting clients
- Teachers or professors
- People in your mom group
- People in your dad group
- People in your Bible study
- People you've met at the gym
- People you've met through hobbies
- People at businesses you visit often: restaurants, coffee shops, grocery stores, gas stations
- Existing contacts: cell phone contacts, Christmas card list
- Social media followers
- Professional contacts: dentist, doctor, realtor, lawn guy, massage therapist, lawyer, accountant, nail technician

The list goes on. Even if you're new to town, you probably have contact with other humans on a daily basis. These are potential clients! A lot of my new-to-town stylists have also learned how to use Facebook groups to network and meet people.

Remember: you don't have to know everyone. You have to have clients who know everyone. The people who have great influence on their circles, who love to share, who were born and raised in your city, who volunteer, who have great hair and want everyone to see it—these people will help you expand your List of Twenty very quickly.

Ask yourself, *Who do I know:*

- who is enthusiastic and loves to share with others?
- who has a great head of hair?
- who works in marketing or social media?
- who would be my dream client?

Contact them. Invite them in for a free or discounted service. Give them a fabulous service. Then watch them help you build your clientele.

BREAKING UP IS HARD TO DO

When I went to cosmetology school, I assumed that if I studied hard in school and landed at a great salon, the clients would come rolling in. My calendar would be full.

Wrong.

What I failed to remember is that everyone has a hairstylist. They had all been getting their hair cut by someone long before I came along. Sitting in my chair meant they would have to break up with their previous stylist in one way or another.

The same is true for you. Every single person you reach out to has a hairstylist. That fact may not matter when you contact your List of Twenty because those friends and family will most likely come see you because they love you. But with everyone else, you need to convince them to "cheat" on their stylist.

Some people have been seeing their stylist for over fifteen years. They exchange Christmas cards and occasionally attend family birthday parties. These are not your clients. Don't waste time trying to break up this marriage. Move on.

There are a ton of people out there who are indifferent about their stylist. They only keep going because the person is less than a mile away or because they don't want to be bothered with finding someone else. These are potential clients. They're open to a switch because they're not committed to the relationship they have.

NO GUARANTEES

Research shows that most people switch salons because of indifference. Essentially, they move on because they didn't have a strongly positive or negative experience, possibly because the service fell flat or the conversation was meh.

Or because the stylist never followed up.

This is an important reminder as you build a clientele: **you are never guaranteed a second visit from a client**. You can never take them for granted and assume they are "yours." This is true throughout your career, but especially at the beginning. People know your work will be evolving; they are coming to see you in school, after all. That means you need to overdo it on customer service, overall experience, and follow up, in addition to honing your skills. That way if they do give you a second shot, their next visit will be exponentially better than the first.

Then there are people who are more than indifferent. They are flat-out unhappy for one reason or another. These are definitely potential clients.

That said, I have one warning: if an unhappy client says something like, "My stylist can *never* get it right" or "I'm on my third stylist this year," beware. When clients are always unhappy or bounce around a lot, the problem is often with the client and not the stylist. You don't want to waste your time on someone who is never satisfied, especially this early in your career.

If you sense someone is hesitant, keep it breezy. You could say something like, "Hey, I don't know if you're married to your hairstylist or not. If you are, I totally get it. But if you're open to a change, I'd love to invite you in for a little special incentive I'm offering to new clients. I know it's a pain to move to a new stylist or salon, so I'd love to give you twenty percent off your first visit. If I could have a full book of clients exactly like you, I'd be a pretty happy hairstylist."

Flatter the person a little bit and give them an incentive, but also keep it wide open for them to say no. If they do say no, follow up with, "Okay, great. Who do you know that might want to come get twenty percent off?"

Don't let that "no" linger. Use it as a way to network and expand your circle.

SOCIAL MEDIA: A PIECE OF THE NETWORKING PIE

I'm going to take a wild guess here: you are on social media. And most likely, your following includes your existing circle of friends and family. That's great! You can use social media as part of your networking plan and as a way to build your business.

There are some specific things to consider when you start using social media as a business-building tool. First, people do business with people they know, like, and trust. So, you have to make sure that on social media you are known, you are likable, and you deliver trustworthy content. That means letting people get to know you in a slightly curated, more professional way than you may have before you started cosmetology school.

Consider your ideal clients (remember that journal entry from Chapter 1?):

- How old are they?
- What do they like to do?
- Where do they hang out?
- What kind of hair do they have?
- What do they find interesting, funny, and share-worthy?
- What do they find boring or cringe-worthy?

Then think about this: How can you serve those people? What content will draw their attention, give them an idea for their own hair, cause them to like and even share your post? When you put out content that serves these people, you will become a magnet for your ideal clients.

Also, make sure you follow people who fall into your ideal clientele and interact with their content. Doing so will feed the algorithm so more of your content ends up in their feed.

WHAT WILL THEY FIND?

While you are in school, you will ultimately be looking for a job. After you submit a résumé, I guarantee your potential employer will google your name and/or search for you on social media.

What will they find?

Even if you only share your hair account on your résumé, your potential employer will most likely find your personal account. If you have questionable content on that account, you have two options: start cleaning it up or make it private before you start sending out résumés.

Your personal account probably has more followers than your hair account, so you might want to focus on managing that account. That's where your people are. Delete photos you don't want a potential boss to see, and start peppering in your hair content.

In Chapters 5 and 6, we'll discuss your personal brand and online presence in detail.

Maybe this sounds familiar: You heard you should have a hair account on Instagram, so you create an account on your first day of school. You take a first-day-of-school photo with your hair styled just so. And then you don't post another photo.

Meanwhile, you post to your personal account every day. You

have thousands of friends and acquaintances. But you're timid about posting your hair pictures there because it's a new journey.

Those thousands of followers? Those are your people! Let them in on the journey. In addition to the List of Twenty, your private account is where you start networking and expanding your circle. Let people get to know you: where you shop, where you eat, what you wear, how you style your hair, how you style others' hair. Some people will see you and think, *Hmm. I like her. I'd love to have her do my hair.*

You have probably grown up with social media and with the mindset of documenting everything: meals, parties, vacations, reunions, hikes, everything. Don't change that habit. Just document in a way that's going to benefit you and expand your circle.

POSTS THAT BUILD YOUR NETWORK

So what should you post? What kind of posts will help you use social media as a networking tool?

- Pictures that show you having fun in school. Show the day-to-day activities: sitting in class with your fellow students or your early mannequin head adventures. Don't just post pictures of finished heads of hair. Show every stage of the process. The more you can showcase that you love what you do, the more your passion will attract people to your chair.
- Post behind-the-scenes photos of your tools and workspace.
- Post before and after pictures, whether you're doing a blowout, cut, or color.
- Post selfies to show what you wear to school, how you style your hair, and so on.
- Post pictures of your life outside school. I'll say it again: let people get to know you. Post pictures with your pets, family, and significant other if you are comfortable sharing. Post photos of vacations

and birthday parties. A word of caution, however: keep the beer-drinking, bikini-wearing photos on your phone and off social media. More on that in Chapter 6.

If social media is an afterthought and you often forget to post, I recommend setting a timer on your phone. Consider your clientele and post at a time when they will be scrolling. If your clientele is the corporate working type, for example, don't post in the middle of the day. Post in the evening when they're home relaxing. If they are fellow moms, post super early when they're checking that feed before they get the kids going. Be intentional and creative.

BE INTENTIONAL

Because we spend so much time on our phones, and because social media is called *social* media, we feel like we're interacting with people when really we're just scrolling through photos and leaving a comment or two. Social media is actually isolating and is not a great way to get to know people.

I'm as guilty as the next person. I know some people exclusively through memes sent over social media. We don't say anything, other than "OMG," "Hilarious!" "LOL." For all I know, they're going through a divorce or one of their kids is getting bullied at school. We're not getting into the nitty-gritty of each other's lives.

Being on our phones also gives us a false sense of productivity. We can scroll for hours (don't believe me? Check your screen time) and leave a few comments, but have we really done anything worthwhile?

The ambitious stylist is intentional about networking, and that includes the use of our phones and social media.

Sarah Cabral is a Balayage Specialist/Educator in Massachusetts. When she started in the industry twenty-two years ago, social media wasn't really a thing. Now that it is, she recommends that apprentices and new stylists take full advantage of it:

Unfortunately, back then we did not have social media, so we would hand out our cards to anyone that we met. My advice for any new stylists is take advantage of social media! The industry has evolved so much and there are so many more opportunities for stylists because of social media. Free education is at your fingertips. Never stop educating yourself! Now we can showcase our work and build a clientele so much easier!

I know you don't have a lot of down time. You might be in school forty hours a week and spend another ten to fifteen hours working nights or weekends. That doesn't leave a lot of time to network and meet people.

So use every interaction you already have. Talk to the people at your part-time job. Talk to the cashier at the grocery store. Talk to the person sitting next to you on the subway or at church. Ask them where they get their hair done. Ask if they want a free blowout or trim.

Even be intentional about the time spent on your phone. Create your List of Twenty. Engage with people who are your ideal clients. Take photos when you're practicing skills and use them to create a story about your hair journey.

In my experience, most students don't network while they're in school. Then they get ready to go on the floor, and they don't have a single client. If you start now with simply creating a List of Twenty or talking to people in the course of your day at the coffee shop or gym, you will be far ahead of the crowd.

No employer expects you to start with three hundred clients.

They know you've been in school. But what if you show up with fifty, twenty, or even ten? You'll be way ahead of most people. Plus, when your new employer says, "Hey, I need you to bring in a model for a highlight," you can immediately say, "I have the girl." You don't have to start from scratch.

Networking requires a mindset shift: you have to see everyone as a potential client. No matter where you go, every person has their hair cut. Opportunities are out there if you simply mention that you are a hairstylist. Be genuine. Be interested in others. But also be willing to put yourself out there. Tell people what you do. You'll be amazed at how the doors fly open.

Leaving business cards at your gym or favorite coffee shop may feel like you're networking, but you're not. No one cares about your business card. They want to meet the person behind the card.

If you become friendly with the girl at the front desk of your gym, offer to give her a blowout. Then she's going to be seen by everyone walking into the gym. If you chat with the same barista every time you get a latte, invite him in for a free trim. Take care of the people who serve as gatekeepers, and they'll help you spread the word.

Think of something you're passionate about and focus on networking with that circle of people. If you volunteer at the Humane Society once a month, get to know the people you volunteer with. If you are active in your church, get to know those who sit in the same pew every Sunday. Lead with authenticity. Be genuine. Networking really is nothing more than getting to know people, expanding your circle, and then asking them to come in for a service in a natural way.

The more you network, the more people you will have in your circle to invite in for a blowout—the gateway to building trust and a solid clientele.

Chapter 4

BLOWOUTS ARE THE GATEWAY

THERE'S NOTHING WORSE THAN GOING TO THE SALON AND spending your hard-earned money and precious time on a cut and dry that leaves you feeling the need to go home and fix it.

Okay, maybe there is something worse: not getting a blowout at all. In college I went to a hairdresser who would shampoo my hair after a color, and then send me to a vanity equipped with blow dryers, brushes, and styling tools so I could finish my own hair. No, thank you.

Done right, blowouts are the cherry on top of any service. When you're new to the industry, however, they can also serve as the gateway to building a strong clientele. After reading this chapter, you'll have tried-and-true tips for delivering the perfect blowout and gaining new clients in the process.

LOW STAKES, HIGH REWARDS

Think about it: blowouts are the lowest-stake service you can provide. It's not like cutting too much hair off or getting the color wrong. What's the worst that can happen if a blowout goes wrong? You rewet the hair and start over. Easy.

There are memes upon memes with dry shampoo jokes and the beauty calculations women use to line up their hair-wash days with events in their social calendar. This is a huge opportunity for the new stylist. You can give people the gift of time, allow them to zone out with a good book, and help them plan their social lives, all while building a clientele base for yourself. Win–win.

As mentioned, most prospective clients already have a stylist. Blowouts are an easy way to invite people to try you out without feeling like they're cheating. They also provide an opportunity to get to know new clients better, chat about products, practice the habit of prebooking, and take photos for social media.

Learning to deliver an excellent blowout now will not only set you apart from your fellow students. It will also make you stand out from other apprentices and impress future employers. Being able to deliver a great finish quickly is money in this industry.

If you learn nothing else from this book, let it be this: **use blowouts, even free ones, to fill out your books, starting now when you're still in school.**

VOICES FROM THE FIELD

Gilbert Garcia managed Mirror Mirror for its first ten years and played an integral role in our growth. He then took a job in Los Angeles at Nine Zero One Salon, an iconic salon that sees a celebrity clientele on a very regular basis.

Here's what he had to say about using blowouts:

> Los Angeles is the land of events and looking your best—always. Who would turn down a free blowout?! I always encourage a new apprentice (or even a new stylist looking to build their book) to invite prospective new clients in for a free blowout. The overhead is minimal and all it costs you is your time! That's your chance to wow them, make an impression, and get them in your chair again for a color or cut service and spread the word!

If your school won't let you offer complimentary blowouts to build your clientele, give the administrators this book. Then decide if you will pay the cost yourself or pitch affordable blowouts to your family and friends. Chances are the going rate will be worth it for you and your clients.

You have to be clocked in anyway, right? Might as well use your time to hone your blowout skills on people who could become clients when you're out of school.

Or you can punch the clock and sit around waiting for the front desk to hand you a ticket with *Perm* or *Pedicure* written on it.

INVITE, INVITE, INVITE

In Chapter 3, we talked about creating your List of Twenty and then coming up with targeted invitations to get each person in for a free or discounted service. As mentioned, the blowout is the least risky of your service options. So, come up with multiple invitations since blowouts are what you will most likely sell to prospective clients.

For example, depending on the situation, you could text the following, or say it as part of a conversation:

- "Hey, I have a little time on X date at X time. I'd love to show you the salon. Want to pop by for a blowout? My treat."
- "Oh my goodness. You should totally come in and get a free blowout. I'd love to do it. How about X date at X time?"
- "Do you have a big social event coming up, like a wedding or party? Let's get you in for a blowout a couple of days before."
- "The other day you mentioned how stressed work has been. Want to come in for a head massage and blowout? It's so relaxing. How about X date at X time?"

You can also use social media. You might post a slide with something like, "I have room for three people to come in for a free blowout this week. DM me if you want one of the slots." Or "I have room for a blowout on Tuesday at ten o'clock. Who wants it?" See who bites. You might get a response from someone you didn't think of inviting in. Add her to your List of Twenty!

When you book these slots, post the slide again and write, "Booked!" so your followers know they better act quick the next time you post a special. You want to make it look like you're busy, even when you're still in school and building your books.

Here's another way to use social media in conjunction with your direct invitations: post pictures of great blowouts. Let people see the amazing work you're doing. The person who received the service is likely to come back, and maybe even ask for a trim. People online might jump a little more quickly the next time you post an availability. During this time in school, you're building trust, so show people what you can do.

Journal Challenge

Now you have some scripts to use when you invite friends and family in for a blowout. The next question is, who will you invite? Use your journal to brainstorm ten people you can bring in for a blowout.

BLOWOUT TIPS AND TRICKS

So, how do you give the perfect blowout? It starts with remembering that this service is much more than simply washing and blow drying someone's hair. Many people get so wrapped up in the actual blow dry that they rush through the steps leading up to it. Take your time, and you'll quickly establish yourself as a professional.

1. GET A GAME PLAN

Before you head to the shampoo bowl, talk to your client. Consultation is key, whether you're doing a cut, color, or blowout.

As part of a consultation, I love to ask this one question: "What does your hair not do that you wish it did?"

In all my years as a stylist, I have never had someone say, "Oh, I love my hair. *Everything* about it is perfect!" Everyone has a little something that has always bothered them about their hair. This is your opportunity to fix it.

What happens next is critical. The person needs to know you're listening. They need to hear, "I hear you and I can help."

You might look at the client's hair and think, *Honey, you need some volume,* and plan your service with that in mind. But if she says, "I wish my hair wasn't so frizzy," then you're heading in the wrong direction.

If you listen and hear her top complaint, then you can introduce some products to help with the frizz or whatever she wants to fix. And you've just earned a brand-new client because you did what she wanted.

2. WALK AND TALK

Now you have a game plan. You know the client's desires and the products to help you deliver what she wants. It's time to head to the shampoo bowl.

As you walk over, continue the conversation by asking about products she uses at home: "What shampoo do you use? How are you liking it?"

And then listen. (Yes, listening is a *big* part of this job!) If it's clear that she loves her current shampoo, grab the same product or something similar. If she's indifferent or in the market for something new, then think about her answer when you asked, "What does your hair not do that you wish it did?" Pick a shampoo and conditioner to solve that problem. And then get to work.

3. SHAMPOO AND MASSAGE

Once the client is sitting at the shampoo bowl, the product conversation stops. You can pick it up later, but for now let her relax. Don't talk during this shampoo unless the client asks you a question. This is her time. Let her enjoy it.

The right pressure and a soothing head massage will give her the confidence that you know what you're doing.

4. WRAP AND RETURN

When you're done at the shampoo bowl, wrap the client's hair neatly in a towel and send her back to your chair. Make sure the towel is nice and snug so water doesn't drip down her neck and back.

While she returns to your chair, clean up the shampoo area, return the bottles, and sanitize the bowl.

5. BLOW DRY

Think back to the client's answer to your first question: "What does your hair not do that you wish it did?" Now is your chance to deliver the solution.

> **VOICES FROM THE FIELD**
>
> Clint Torres, Celebrity Stylist at Nine Zero One Salon in Los Angeles, has this tip for a bomb blowout:
>
> Slow down. Let the blow dryer do its job. Try five passes instead of ten passes per section. It looks professional, it's less pulling on the client's hair, and it's efficient.

Use your fingers to manipulate the hair while you're power drying—either lifting it up for volume or using tension to start smoothing, especially around the hairline. Then, when the hair is nearly dry, pick up your brush and finish the job.

MAKING MAGIC

Aim to master three general styles:

- Bouncy, nineties, voluminous
- Smooth, sleek, straight
- Short pixies

In all three cases, make sure you power dry the hair before you start round brushing. Most of the magic happens when the hair is at least 90 percent dry, so resist the urge to start styling too soon.

As you work, talk about the products you're using. Tell the client why you chose this or that product and what problem it will solve. If you're using products that do multiple things, like heat protection and smoothing, even better.

Also use this time to ask questions about their hair, for example:

- If you can tell they color their hair: "Who colors your hair?"
- If they don't color their hair: "Have you ever thought about a few highlights around your face for summer?"
- Anyone: "When was the last time you got a haircut?"

These questions plant seeds for future visits.

When you're finished, get feedback by asking questions like, "What do you think?" or "Do you like it?" or "Is there anything we need to change?" Don't feel like you have to ask all three. If you do, you'll run the risk of sounding insecure about your work.

Their expression and body language alone will tell you whether they are happy, but you still want to ask these types of questions. You want to be confident they are pleased and will tell others.

How will you know if the client isn't happy? Believe me, you'll know. She'll start messing with her hair, flipping the part to the opposite side, or pulling sections this way and that. She'll give very short answers, and she probably won't be smiling.

If you notice these cues, ask, "Is there anything I can do for you?" And if worse comes to worse, you simply start over with a wash and then re-dry. Remember, it's a low-stakes service.

More often than not, when you finish, the client will say something like, "I wish I could take you home with me" or "I wish I had planned a date night" or "I wish I had makeup on now that my hair is done." Those are all great indicators that she is happy, and that she might be your next cut or color client.

As you walk the person to the front, show her the products you used so she knows exactly what she needs to buy to re-create the look she loves. Tell her you would love to see her again, either for another blowout or maybe for a trim or highlights. Also ask if she knows anyone else who would be interested in a free blowout.

If someone is indifferent or downright unhappy, talk to her about the products, check her out, and let it go. You can't please everyone. Focus on the people who are practically wagging their tails because they're so happy. Those are your potential long-term clients.

FORTUNE IN THE FOLLOW-UP

A couple days after the blowout, follow up with something like, "Hey, I just wanted to follow up and say thank you so much for coming in. Hopefully your blowout lasted a few days. I would love to see you in the future for a cut or color. And if you know anyone who would love to get a free blowout, let me know. Any friend of yours is a friend of mine."

Also, try to bring up something you talked about so your thank-you text doesn't look copy and pasted. For example, "I hope you had a great time on your vacation!"

If you talked about cutting and coloring, bring that up as well: "You mentioned that you were due for a trim in a few weeks. I have an opening on X day at X o'clock. Let me know if you want it."

Another tip: Give people a choice of two yeses, for example, "Remind me: do you usually go six weeks or eight weeks on your color? I have an opening on X day at X o'clock or X day at X o'clock. Which one works better?"

What if the person doesn't take you up on this offer? If the person falls into the category of ideal customer, don't be shy about sending another invitation after the thank-you text. People know you're in school. They know you're trying to build a clientele.

In addition, your ideal client probably hangs out with other ideal clients. So, you could offer her an opportunity to participate in a referral program: "In a perfect world I'd have a full clientele of people exactly like you. Send me your friends, and I'll give you five dollars off for each person who comes in."

Asking for referrals is nerve-racking, I know. It probably feels like you're begging. But if you've already established that this person really liked the blowout you provided, why wouldn't she want her friends to get the same service?

Plus, asking for referrals is something you'll do even five, ten, fifteen years into your career. You should always have the mindset of growing your network and building your clientele. Might as well build that muscle now.

For those non-tail waggers who seemed either indifferent or unhappy: follow up with them too. For all you know, that person always has RBF (wink) or is quiet and nonexpressive by nature. She may have loved the blowout even if it didn't seem like it. She may have been having a bad day. You just never know. So don't miss the opportunity to follow up. That person could end up being one of your 20 percent.

If you do your follow-ups by phone, you may get more information from people who seemed unhappy but didn't say anything. Here's how that conversation might go:

"Hi, I'm just checking in to see how you liked your blowout. We also talked about you coming in for a trim."

"Well, if I'm being honest, it didn't hold."

"Oh, no problem. Let me have you in to try again. Does X day at X time work?"

Some people don't say what they're really thinking when they're sitting in the chair because it's awkward. By following up, you give them an opportunity to tell you what happened—rather than telling their friend or going to another stylist. That follow-up gives you a chance to save the relationship and add a new client to your books. *The ambitious stylist is always open to feedback.*

QUANTITY, THEN QUALITY

When you're in school, it's important to focus on the quantity of services. Get as many people as possible to come in to have you work on their hair. Chances are, you will sell more people on blowouts, compared to cuts or colors, because it's so low risk. Take advantage of the opportunity to put a bunch of beautiful walking billboards out into the world. With repetition, your quality will improve as well.

Don't get me wrong: you should still take your time and put effort into quality work on each person, but don't get so hung up on quality that you miss out on the opportunity for lots of repetition.

Doing all of these blowouts also gives you a chance to practice delivering world-class hospitality. The service itself is only part of it. You also need to work on prebooking the next appointment, talking about and educating on the products used, and taking a picture to share on social media. If you rinse and repeat with every client, these steps will become habits you do without even thinking about it.

ASK FOR PERMISSION

Even though taking selfies and posting photos on social media is natural for almost everyone, ask clients before you take a photo and post it on Instagram. Just in case.

Are you excited about using blowouts to build your clientele? You should be. It really is the easiest way to go about it, and it's something you can start right now.

Bringing your List of Twenty and others in for a blowout is an excellent way to build your confidence too. Confidence in your hair-handling skills, as well as your ability to hold a conversation, make people feel comfortable, and practice the three Ps: prebook, product, picture.

Your clients shouldn't be the only ones getting a blowout. You need to blow out, or at least style, your own hair every day, no matter where you're going. Why? Your hair is the biggest part of your personal brand—the way you sell yourself as a stylist.

Chapter 5

PERSONAL BRAND

HAVE YOU NOTICED THAT EVERYONE HAS A WATER BOTTLE THESE days? It's a thing. There's YETI. Hydro Flask. Nalgene. CamelBak. Stanley. They come in colors like lupine, tiger lily, and electric magenta, as well as the more basic black and charcoal. You can even customize your lid with a flip-up straw, screw-on cap, slide, push button, or push-pull.

So many varieties, and yet they all serve the same purpose: they carry liquid.

So what sets one apart from the other? Why would someone proudly carry their YETI in their backpack or tote their Stanley everywhere they go? It all comes down to branding.

Let's take Nalgene, for example. In my opinion, the lid is annoying—it flops in your face if you don't hold it down while you drink. Plus the bottle barely keeps water cold. In many ways, it's not practical.

Why would some use a Nalgene despite these issues? My guess is they want to identify with the brand. It's their thing. They want people to see them as healthy and eco-conscious because they drink copious amounts of water from a thirty-two-ounce BPA-free bottle made from 50 percent recycled material.

The cool part about a brand is that it can change. It doesn't have to be permanent. Stanley, for example, has been around since 1913. For most of those one hundred years, the color of their water bottles was a basic army green. No rose quartz or pool or chambray.

Then they decided to make a change. It wasn't inauthentic. They simply made a conscious decision to shift their brand to go with the times while maintaining their quality product.

Why am I talking about water bottles? Because like Stanley, Nalgene, and the rest, you have a brand—a style, a vibe, a way of showing up with others. In a service industry, your brand is a key piece of building the clientele you want.

In this chapter, we'll talk about what a personal brand is, why you should care about it, and how you can intentionally build it in a way that sets you apart and attracts your ideal clients.

WHAT IS YOUR BRAND?

At the most basic level, personal brand is your vibe. It's the way you talk, dress, and carry yourself. It includes your hair, makeup, facial expressions, and body language. The way you speak to and about others. The impression you leave on people. It includes your core beliefs and values, as those come out in your actions and speech, both in person and online.

You are training for a job in an aesthetic industry. That means, for better or worse, outward appearance plays a big role. Not that you have to dress a certain way or have a certain hairstyle. You simply need to make a conscious choice to present yourself in a way that is consistently and authentically you.

As the saying goes, your vibe attracts your tribe. Since you're trying to attract dream clients and soon a dream home salon, you have to really think about the impression you're putting out there.

LOOK IN THE MIRROR

Time for a reality check: Go stand in front of a mirror. Look at yourself as if you are a prospective client. Then ask yourself, "Would I want to spend several hours with this person? Let her touch my hair? Hand her lots of money?"

If the answer is no, ask yourself why. Do you look sloppy? Is it obvious you stayed out all night? Are you clearly overdue for a mani or highlight? Did you forgo your makeup?

I know you're in school. You might be waitressing at night. You're tired. It's easy to get into the habit of rolling out of bed, throwing on your uniform, pulling your hair into a messy ponytail, and heading out the door, with or without makeup.

But is that how you want to present yourself? Is that your personal brand of choice?

You may say, "Oh, I won't dress like that when I have a job. I'll take more time to do my hair and makeup."

That may be true, but remember this: You're building a clientele *now*. You're inviting your List of Twenty in for a blowout *now*. That means you have to start working on that brand *now*.

WEEKEND GIRL

Time for another reality check: Think about the girl who goes out on the weekend and socializes with her friends. What does she look like? How does she dress? How about her makeup and hair? How does she treat others?

Now, think about the girl who comes to class during the week. What does she look like? How does she dress? How about her makeup and hair? How does she treat others?

If you're like most students, you probably need to bring a little more of that weekend girl into the classroom.

It drives me crazy when I see my apprentices looking all cute and pulled together on social media, when they don't put that kind of effort into how they show up at the salon. There's a mismatch in personal brand. The lack of effort shows laziness and no attention to detail, and that's not the vibe you want to give your employer or client.

SOCIAL MEDIA CHECK

Reality check number three: Look at your Instagram account. What do you see in the first nine pictures? Does that brand match what's on display day to day?

Let's say your Instagram hair account is styled in the blush tones of some blogger preset you bought because you thought that's what you should do as a stylist. In real life, however, you're a rocker. You wear black T-shirts, ripped jeans, and boots. Soft blush tones versus black tees—that's a major disconnect from a style perspective. Neither is right or wrong, but they are very different and will attract a very different clientele.

Here's a news flash: Your brand is always on. Online or in person, it's all you, and it all needs to line up. You are now in a constant state of finding clients, so you want to project the same personal brand no matter where you are.

That said, don't overthink it. Your brand should come naturally.

You're not putting on a mask. You're putting forth the best version of yourself. So, consider who you are and who you want to be, and work toward making those match wherever you are—online, in school, with friends and family. Be authentically you.

PEERS CHECK

At the annual Mirror Mirror holiday party, we give out Culture Awards. Before the event, everyone votes on who they think best represents each of the company's core values, and then we announce the winners at the party.

The funny thing is that in every single category, the winner is almost always a slam dunk. When asked who best represents Fun or Fresh or Welcoming, almost everyone thinks of the same person.

Why? Because personal brand is obvious. People know. They pick up on how we dress, how we act and talk, how we show up day after day.

Think about it this way: If a good friend were to dress up as you for Halloween, would they know what to wear? Probably, right down to your trucker hat or Dunks. They would be able to mimic the way you greet people, the way you lean in and touch someone's arm when you're talking, your encouraging comments (or your constant complaining and gossip?), your loud laugh, your empathetic nodding.

If you want to get a good sense of your personal brand as it currently stands, ask a few close friends: Do they see you as shy and quiet? Loud and outgoing? Trendy and fashion-forward? Perfectionistic? Laid-back? A combination of these?

Now is the time to consciously think about how you show up. You might discover you're not thrilled with what you find. That's okay! School is the perfect place to start figuring it out. You can start leaning into what you like and begin changing what you don't like. The next section can help build the brand that is authentically you.

HOW TO BUILD YOUR BRAND

As mentioned, your personal brand is made up of several things: clothing style, hair and makeup, personality, actions, words, attitudes, and more. As a stylist, it also includes your skills.

UNCOVER YOUR SUPERPOWER

In the book *Good to Great*, Jim Collins talks about the importance of figuring out one's superpower: what can you be the best in the world at?

That's great advice for you as a stylist too. What is your superpower? In a room of one hundred stylists, what will you be known for? Here are a few ideas to get the creative juices flowing:

- Dimensional color that last six months
- Precise highlights on blondes

- Platinum blondes
- Fashion colors
- Natural redheads
- Corrective color
- Funky festival hair
- Avant garde, artsy runway looks
- Extensions
- Textured hair
- Set work
- Bridal work/updos

We've already talked about using your time in school to learn what services you like doing and which ones you're especially good at. Let this be another reminder to find that superpower! It's an essential part of your personal brand as a stylist.

As you start figuring it out, start showcasing your superpower on social media. That way, when you apply for your dream job, your future employer will see the continuity between in person and online. And if you've found a place that is truly a perfect fit, the interviewer will walk away with the sense that you already work there.

LOOK IN THE MIRROR, TAKE TWO

Here's another mirror exercise: Think about the last time you stood in front of the mirror and thought, *Okay, there she is!* A time when you felt your best. Your hair, your outfit, your whole presence felt right and you left the house feeling comfortable and confident.

What were you wearing? Bright colors? Ripped jeans? Cute sneakers? How had you styled your hair? Did you do anything different with your makeup?

Figure out what it was that gave you that comfortable, confident feeling, and turn that into the "uniform" aspect of your personal brand. Make that outfit your thing, dialed up or down depending on the occasion. For me, that uniform is a chambray shirt with cute denim (a.k.a. a Canadian tuxedo) and some fun sneakers. It looks pulled together, and it's so easy and comfortable.

Some of you may already have a strong sense of style. You know your go-to outfit is a funky T-shirt with combat boots, or a denim jacket over a comfy dress, or a cute hat with your signature long hair, or bright red lips with an all-black outfit. You get the idea. Some of you may have to think a little harder about your style, but you still probably have a general sense.

In either case, building your brand involves consciously thinking about how you show up, and possibly changing your look and demeanor if you realize it's not what you want to put out there—especially in the salon.

I hate that outward appearance is so important in our industry, but that's the deal. The sooner you accept it and embrace it, the better. Just like you don't go to a dentist with bad teeth, you don't go to a stylist with bad hair and apparently no concern for what she looks like. So, decide what your appearance brand is and intentionally own it every day.

As stated, your brand involves more than just your clothes and hair. It also includes your words and actions. What is your superpower in this realm? Are you the friendly one? The funny one? The helpful one? Not that you can't be more than one of these, but what contribution do you most naturally and authentically make to the lives of others?

Start paying attention to how you interact with your family, friends, and fellow students. In particular, pay attention to how others respond. When do they appear relaxed and happy? Lean into your actions and words that make people feel good about themselves.

You've already been putting out this brand, this impression, whether consciously or not. Now you need to shift your mindset. Ambitious stylists *intentionally* craft their brand. They know what they're putting out into the world through their appearance, words, and actions. They think about how they dress and engage with others.

The more specific your brand, the better. It must be dialed in everywhere—at a friend's bachelorette party, at the gym, in class. You are a walking advertisement for your services as a stylist.

That may sound exhausting, but it gets easier. Once you become established and have a full clientele, you won't have to work quite as hard. It will become second nature. Plus, if your brand is authentically you, living it 24/7 won't be such a chore.

Journal Challenge

I could write a whole book on personal brand, and each of the following categories could have its own chapter.

For now, I'm giving you a brief checklist to remind you to consider each of these aspects of your brand. For each one, ask yourself, (1) What is my brand in this area? (2) Is that the brand I want? (3) If not, what changes can I make?

Remember: your vibe attracts your tribe! Be specific and honest about where you are and where you want to be.

- My stylist superpower:
- My clothing style:
- My hair style:
- My makeup style:
- My personality strength:

START NOW

It takes seven seconds to make a first impression. That's less time than it takes to sing the first line of "Twinkle Twinkle Little Star." And you only get one chance to make a first impression, so best to get it right.

It's important to make a good first impression in any situation, but especially when you're applying for a job. And your first impression starts long before you're sitting in front of an interviewer. It starts now.

How you dress, speak, and act. Your hair and makeup. What you post on Instagram. Your sense of humor. Your thoughtful compliments. All of these things play into the impression you give people. As a stylist, this impression includes your service superpowers—your color, cutting, or specialty service skills. Take time to intentionally create and maintain an impression, a brand, that is authentically and consistently you.

Your brand should represent the real you, not a fake ideal or something you think you should be. If your brand is put on, at some point that mask will fall off. Make it easy on yourself.

Be you. With everyone. All the time. *The ambitious stylist is authentic and showcases a consistent brand to friends, coworkers, and clients.*

This is the best way to attract the right clients and the right salon. This is the best way to set yourself up for success.

Maybe you did the exercises in this chapter and realized you don't like what you see. Maybe your brand is inconsistent or not what you want it to be as a stylist. Be like Stanley and change it! Make a complete 180 if you want. Start now, while you're in school, so that you are fully living it online and in person by the time you start applying for jobs.

In the next chapter, we'll focus on one specific part of your brand: your online presence.

Chapter 6

ONLINE PRESENCE

WHEN SOMEONE WANTS TO WORK AT MIRROR MIRROR, THEY FILL out an application that comes directly to my inbox. At the bottom of the page, I ask people to include their social media handle "so we can get to know one another."

The first thing I do after I open the document is click on that social media account. And I can pretty much guarantee I'm not the only salon owner who does this.

What does that tell you? Your online presence is *very* important.

I've now reviewed over five hundred applications, and based on responses to a few questions and what I find on social media, I can almost always identify the people who will be a good fit.

At the same time, I know I've probably missed out on some excellent stylists because the vibe they gave on Instagram and TikTok was a great fit for another salon, but not for Mirror Mirror. They missed out on a chance to interview because of a mismatch in brand—a brand they may not even realize they're putting out there.

In this chapter, I want to help you avoid disqualifying yourself from your dream salon because of your online presence. We'll talk about some positive and negative social media examples, and look at tips for cleaning up the online presence you didn't know you have. I'll also include a few "voices from the field" so you can learn from people who have been in your shoes.

VOICES FROM THE FIELD

Brynn Reed, the Lead Extension Specialist at Mirror Mirror, has been in the industry for fifteen years. Here's her advice related to online presence:

> As a new stylist, an online presence is imperative; it is the perfect way you can make yourself stand out from the other applicants.
>
> One great way I was able to build my online presence was utilizing a "model day." I would pick one day a week and grab a couple friends that are comfortable in front of the camera. I would style their hair to showcase the color/cut/extensions I had created for them and get great content to post on social media! Now that you have some beautiful pictures of your work that are congruent with your personal brand, your potential employer will be able to see exactly what you're capable of and the kind of work that you produce.

WHAT IS YOUR ONLINE PRESENCE?

Time for another reality check: put down this book, pick up your phone, and google yourself.

What did you find?

If you're straight out of high school, you might not find much. That's actually better than finding a bunch of things you're not especially proud of.

If you have a common name, you might find a lot of information about someone else. And unfortunately, the other Sarah Smith might be a convicted felon with an unattractive mugshot or two. Nothing you can do about that, other than be aware and make sure *your* presence is exactly what you want it to be.

Next question: does your online presence match your personal brand, and more importantly, does it match the brand you want to intentionally create as a stylist?

If not, that's okay. That's why you're reading this book. The next sections have tips for cleaning up your online presence and intentionally creating the one you want.

CLEAN UP

Whether your online presence is not what it should be, or is not you, or is you but you don't want it to be you, all is not lost. You have time to clean things up while you're still in school so your brand and presence are all aligned before you start applying for jobs.

First, view your online presence as part of your job application. A future employer is looking at these photos. They don't want to see a lot of cleavage or butt cheeks. They don't want to see a beer in your hand in every other photo. They don't want to see you making out with someone or sleeping off a hangover. They don't want to see sloppy hair, sloppy clothes, sloppy behavior.

I know. Some of you are probably rolling your eyes and thinking, *This is 2024!* These guidelines don't mean you should be sitting up straight with your hands folded in your lap, wearing a long-sleeved shirt and maxi skirt. Just use common sense. Pretend your parents are viewing each and every photo.

After you take stock of your photos, start deleting whatever doesn't serve you. It's not enough to create a hair account and keep that one clean. Salon owners will find your personal account, trust me.

OUT WITH THE BAD, IN WITH THE GOOD

When it comes to cleaning up internet search results, there isn't much you can do without reaching out to specific websites. However, you can add new, on-brand content to your own website and social media feeds so the less favorable results move down the list.

Don't have a website? You can use tools such as Squarespace, Wix, Canva, and Milkshake to create one fairly easily. Then load it up with photos that showcase your work, and use as many keywords as possible in the website text—for example, keywords that include your name, job, and location. The website templates usually include a Contact page so you can collect inquiries and client emails—added bonus.

INTENTIONALLY CREATE

In addition to cleaning up the presence you currently have, you need to intentionally create something new and more accurate going forward.

First, create a hair account on Instagram and/or TikTok where you can showcase your art, talent, and (professional) personality. The goal here is to set yourself up as an expert, even if you just started school. Post hair pictures that show your skills and the type of service you want to do. Post pictures of the latest hair trends, like Cowgirl Copper, or the Old Money Bob, or Birkin Bangs. Show people what it's like to be in school, working on doll heads and having fun with your classmates.

Because TikTok tends to be more fun and casual, your posts can be less reserved, but they should still be professional. The same rules apply: don't put any content you wouldn't want a future employer or client to see.

Whichever platforms you use, use social media to paint a picture of who you are. If you've done your other homework, then you know what brand you want to put out there. You know what kind of salon you want to work at, probably someplace where people with a similar brand work.

Knowing those two things, you can intentionally create your online presence to match your brand and the culture of your ideal salon. A prospective salon owner should be able to look at your pictures and think, *She looks like she works here!*

Remember: Be authentic. Show the real you. You don't want a salon owner to think you're a perfect fit and then meet you in person and find out you're not.

Still not sure where to start? Follow other stylists who seem to have a similar mindset and brand. Take note of what they post, the kinds of pictures they take, how they showcase the haircuts or extensions they've done, the kinds of selfies they post, what they're wearing, and so on. You'll gain a lot of ideas on how to intentionally create the brand you want to be known for.

Also, read on. The next section provides real-life examples of online presence—both intentionally and unintentionally created.

I asked Evan McDonald, the Social Media Manager at Mirror Mirror, for some tips on using social media. Here's what she shared:

1. In the beginning it's important to post consistently. As your skills improve and you look back on those posts, saying, "I can do better than that now," that's when you can archive those posts.
2. As important as consistency is, it's also important to post the hair you want in your chair. As in, if you don't want funky cuts or fashion color, don't post it. The salon you apply to is looking at your Instagram for what kind of stylist you want to be, and future clients are looking at your Instagram to see if you can create the hair they want.
3. A common mistake I see among new hair Instagrams is seeming to have rushed the process on taking a picture. These are models and they got an excellent price, so ask them to come to where the lighting is best, pose them, take a million pictures. Also don't forget that in the beginning when you're still learning the perfect cut and color that styling is your best friend with these photos: make it a smooth, shiny blowout, and curl if necessary.
4. Another common mistake I see is the client taking up half the photo. The photo should be of the hair, not half background of the salon and half hair. You want the hair to take up a lot more than 50 percent of the photo.
5. You may be a cosmetology student at the time you're creating your hair Instagram, but the clients will see you the way you present yourself. Make your accounts professional. You can tag your school and celebrate when you graduate, but don't constantly remind your followers that you're a student. Find other stylists' accounts that you like and try to take pointers from them.

A TALE OF THREE APPLICANTS

Perhaps you're still not convinced that online presence is a big deal.

Let me share how I went through the following applicants' social media and what I noticed as a salon owner and employer. Then you can do another reality check against your own online presence and see how it compares.

APPLICANT 1: ABBY

The first thing I noticed was that "Abby's" username was unprofessional and more of a description (I'm leaving out the actual username to protect the guilty). I'm guessing this was her personal Instagram account, but even a personal account should contain a real name if you are intentionally creating an online presence and looking for a job. Your name is the most basic piece of who you are.

In addition, the name given in Abby's profile was different from the username and was also not her real name. The only place Abby's first name appeared was in the link that led to a service booking site.

Next I looked at the bio. Instead of being straightforward, Abby's profile made vague statements like "Entrepreneur," "Popular Loner," and "Original First Class." Nothing about being a hairstylist.

Then I looked below her profile at the highlights section. Personally, I like seeing a few highlights. If you're a student seeking a stylist job, even your personal account highlights should showcase hair in some way. Maybe one highlight shows your weekend life, one shows your hobbies or family life, one shows scenes from school, and one shows examples of your work.

Abby had one highlight. It was a slide she copied from another user and had nothing to do with hair or her personal life.

After scanning her one highlight, I looked at the photos in Abby's feed. Of her thirty most recent posts, twenty-six were selfies, most of which showed Abby wearing a similar unsmiling expression.

What did that tell me about her brand? A few things, actually.

1. **Abby is self-centered, not others-centered.** There's nothing wrong with selfies mixed in with pictures of models showing off a haircut and photos with friends. But this is a service industry.

We focus on others. I don't need to see pictures of the applicant serving dinner at a homeless shelter, but I should see pictures of people other than the applicant.

2. **Abby doesn't come off as a people person.** She had the same pouty and/or unhappy expression in almost every photo. Her profile picture was adorable, and she wore a beautiful smile in a few of the selfies—in these shots she looked friendly and approachable. In most, however, she did not. She looked like she might hurt someone. This isn't a good fit in an industry that focuses on making others feel comfortable.

3. **Abby is not detail oriented.** I could tell that she didn't look into Mirror Mirror before she applied. If she had, she would have known that her sullen demeanor did not match our culture. Even a quick glance at our website would have shown Abby that although we have a lot of different styles—tats, no tats, jeans, skirts, bright colors, all black—everyone has one thing in common: they exude joy. Their expressions and body language show that they genuinely love taking care of people. And they are wildly ambitious. This is not what Abby exuded.

I also saw a disconnect in personal brand. Was Abby the smiling, friendly looking girl I saw in her profile pic, or was she the girl who looked like she wanted to kick my butt? I want to have a pretty good idea of what someone's like before I invite them for an interview.

PERSONAL ACCOUNT TIPS

As mentioned, creating a professional hair account is important. However, you should use your personal account as well. Right now, that's where your people are.

Start peppering your feed with hair photos or pics of you and your classmates. Start building interest and credibility with the circle you already have. That will help you build a clientele.

If you just can't bring yourself to delete questionable photos from your personal account, then change the setting to private—at least while you're going through the interview process. That way you don't inadvertently disqualify yourself from getting an interview. I, for one, am impressed that someone is smart enough to make their account private.

If you set your personal account to private, make sure your hair account shows more than just hair and has enough photos to paint a picture of who you are. Let the employer get to know you and feel confident enough that your brand is a good fit for the salon.

APPLICANT 2: MADISON

The Instagram account Madison (that's her real name; I wanted to give her credit!) provided in her application was clearly related to hair. Her username included her first name, and then her full name appeared in her profile. In addition, the first line of her profile said plainly "future hairstylist" and gave her location.

Under her profile, Madison had six highlights, each one related to hair: client selfies, prices/services, before/after, and more.

In her feed, Madison showcased pictures of clients' hair. No personal, unhappy selfies here. Because this was her hair account, every photo showed work she'd done, whether it was a cut or color.

You might be thinking, *Well, she must have been working already.*

She had experience doing this kind of thing before she applied to Mirror Mirror.

Nope. Madison did all of this while she was a student.

This showed me she is ambitious. She was not wasting time in school. She learned how to do hair *and* take great photos to showcase it.

After checking out Madison's hair account, I searched for her personal account. Here I got a better sense of who she is. Out of the first thirty photos, seven were selfies—compared to Abby's twenty-six.

Mixed in were photos at a wedding, baby shower, and birthday party, as well as photos with her significant other and various groups of people. In every photo Madison was smiling. She appeared friendly and approachable.

One thing that stood out with Madison is that her hair and personal accounts both showed history. I could see that she was the same person over time. I could see the work she was doing over time. What often happens is that someone starts cosmetology school and creates a hair account. They take a first-day-of school photo and maybe one or two classroom shots. And that's it.

Teaching moment: one of the worst things you can do is start a hair account and then only have two pictures. Add pictures regularly. Set a reminder on your phone if you need to. Build your feed.

Madison followed this advice. She clearly had a habit of posting photos. This showed me she had discipline. Anyone can get excited about social media and post regularly for a week or two, but it takes discipline to create a habit of creating content week after week, month after month.

From searching both of her accounts, I felt like I knew Madison. I saw her family, friends, and dog. I saw her clients. Because she took mirror selfies, I could see her outfits and style. From all of this, I could tell her brand matched our own, so I invited her in for an interview.

When I finally met Madison in person, I was not disappointed. Her online presence matched her in-person brand, and she was a perfect fit for Mirror Mirror.

I asked Madison how she looked at posting on her two Instagram accounts. Here's what she said:

When posting on my personal Instagram, I *always* remembered the importance of the internet blueprint and how everything you post can be saved/used by others. I also always thought about my future when posting, so always keeping it professional for future employers and clients but still showing my fun personality! I've dreamed of one day having a good social media follower count, so I think that's played a big role as well; people get "canceled" for things they posted or said ten years ago.

As for my hair Instagram, I made it a priority when I was in hair school to know good hair poses and make them easy and comfortable for clients to do. A cohesive, branded Instagram is so important. I posted everything, and it's always the best feeling when new clients bring in inspo pics off of my own Instagram because everything looks well executed. I am very particular about my hair and can't blame anyone for being that way, so the more I had to post *bomb* hair, the more people would trust me, and the more clientele I got and kept! I studied professional hairstylists' pages to look at lighting, angles, and content for ideas for my own. Being consistent helps with keeping clients engaged. I also was a social media manager before going to cosmetology school and love to have fun on Canva—I always get compliments on my creativity, so just having a page where I could be creative and show my work was something I thrived with.

APPLICANT 3: CHLOE

While Abby is probably the worst example of online presence I've seen in an applicant, Madison is the best. Most applicants, however, fall somewhere in between. That was the case with "Chloe."

I went to speak at a cosmetology school. Afterward, Chloe came up to introduce herself, which was smart and showed ambition. However, she didn't have any makeup on and she was wearing her hair in a messy ponytail. No effort to look put together.

Another teaching moment: you never know who's coming into your school. Someone from your dream salon might come in to speak when you look like you just rolled out of bed. Personal brand every day.

Shortly after, Chloe applied to Mirror Mirror. She had a hair account, and she used her real name as her handle and in her profile. In her profile pic, Chloe looked professional and put together. *Well, who is she?* I thought. *She does know how to bring it.* Completely different from my first impression of her at school. She could have put more effort into posting to this account: she only had thirteen pictures total, and two of them were from her first day in school.

Then I checked her personal account. She had a decent mix of selfies and pictures with others. She smiled a lot, and appeared friendly and approachable. I got the sense that her super casual dress in class was not the norm. Chloe usually looked put together, and her brand seemed to match what we're going for at Mirror Mirror. But oh my, did I see a lot of bathing suit photos!

Overall I was intrigued enough that I invited her in for an interview. Chloe arrived looking like her Instagram photos, confirming my guess that she was just going casual at school. I also knew I could give her the "Martha Lynn Kale Branding Conversation" later—the same conversation I gave you about cleaning up your online presence.

In the end, we did hire Chloe. She was an excellent apprentice and a great culture fit.

ADVICE FOR THE SHY

Are you timid about using social media? Do you hate asking clients if you can take a picture of their hair?

Well, you better get un-timid.

In today's world, you have to be comfortable using social media. If you don't, you'll have a hard time building a clientele. People are so used to googling and checking Yelp for reviews; they're going to do the same in finding a stylist.

You have to put yourself out there a little bit. And don't take yourself too seriously. Have fun with it.

YOU ARE THE LOGO

Let's end this chapter with another reality check.

Take out your phone. Pull up your Instagram account (or TikTok or whatever), and run through the following checklist:

- **Look at your username.** Is it some version of your real name? For example, if it's your hair account, it could be something like Hair by Sarah.
- **Look at your profile pic.** Is it representative of your personal brand? Is your expression welcoming and friendly? Can you see your face, or are you hidden in a group photo or behind big sunglasses?
- **Look at your profile.** Is it straightforward and informative? Does it tell people who you are, what you value? Does your hair account clearly state that you do hair?
- **Look at your feed.** Do the photos give a well-rounded sense of who you are? Is your personal brand clear? Are there photos that

might give a potential employer or client reason to question your professionalism?

- **Check your tagged photos.** Your feed may look curated, but what about your friends' feeds? Make sure you click the tagged photos to see whether others are creating an online presence for you—something that is not representative of what you want communicated to a future employer or client.

A potential employer wants to see the type of person you are and the type of stylist you might be. Potential clients want to see why they should trust you and do business with you. Your username, profile pic, bio, and feed should tell them this.

You are more than just selfies, and you are more than just motivational quotes, and you are more than just pictures of extensions and hair cuts. You are all of the above and more.

I know there are stylists out there who show a lot of skin online and do everything I've said not to do, and they're wildly successful.

But you're not them. At least not yet.

You're just starting out. Until you have a full clientele ready to pay you a bunch of money, you'll make it much easier on yourself if you play by the rules I've suggested. You'll get to that full clientele, high-paying job, and dream life a lot faster.

Still, you may decide that you're different. After reading my recommendations about cleaning up your online presence, covering up that cleavage, and deleting those drinking photos, some of you might be tempted to toss this book in the trash and ignore everything I've said.

You can do that.

But chances are you'll make life harder on yourself. You may not get hired by your dream salon. Instead of being on track to six figures, you may find yourself struggling—or you may have quit because you can't keep a full clientele.

Yes, being a hairstylist is fun and artistic, but it's still a business. Like every business, you have to create a professional aesthetic and brand. If you treat it like a hobby, it will pay like a hobby. If you treat it like a professional career, you'll enjoy much higher returns.

Journal Challenge

I know all this talk about online presence can feel overwhelming and maybe like it's overkill. You may not know where to start. You may feel a touch of analysis paralysis. Or you may brush off all of my advice because "who cares." The worst thing you can do is nothing!

Consider the last time you met a new friend or potential boyfriend. Did you not immediately go to their social media? Of course you did. And most likely the person went to yours.

That's a social setting, where the consequences are fairly minor. Now think about how critical online presence is in a professional setting. Do the work now so it can do the work for you later!

What do you need to do after reading this chapter?

- Do you need to set aside time to review and delete some of your more "revealing" pics?
- Do you need to start showing people more of your cosmetology school journey?
- Do you need to post fewer selfies and more hair pics or photos with family and friends?
- Do you need to post more consistently?

After you think about your next steps, write out your commitment. For example, "I am committed to posting five hair photos per week" or "I will set an alarm on my phone to remind me to post."

To take it a step further, tell someone about your commitment and then do it!

In Chapter 2, I shared my assumptions about those of you reading this book. One is that you are ambitious. You want to get an apprenticeship at a successful salon so that you can learn and grow. These guidelines will get you there in the shortest time possible.

It's hard enough to build a clientele, earn a steady income, and hone your skills. Don't make it harder on yourself by ignoring your online presence. *The ambitious stylist will do the work now so she can focus on her craft once she lands a job.*

Just as you have an online presence, so does every salon. Don't wait till you graduate to start putting your dream into action. Start your salon search now.

Chapter 7

SALON SEARCH

IN COSMETOLOGY SCHOOL, I HAD THE OPPORTUNITY TO WORK with a celebrity stylist who was a big deal in the 1990s. It wasn't really an apprenticeship. I was more like a glorified maid. I checked clients in, swept hair, and helped at the shampoo bowls.

At the time I didn't understand that I could have had a proper apprenticeship with someone who was invested in my education— someone who paid attention to my work and gave me feedback so I could succeed on my own. As a result, I decided to skip the apprenticeship after graduation and went straight for a stylist position. I found a small six-chair commission-based salon. The owner was never around. No one told me how to fill my time or what I should be doing to fill my books. So I relied on the ambition instilled in me by my mom, as well as what I learned in school and in my corporate job. I focused on marketing, marketing, marketing.

It paid off, because ten months into my career, I was a finalist for Best Hairstylist in Austin through Austin Fashion Week.

But this freaked me out. I might be good at marketing myself, but I was still so new in my career. I hadn't really been coached by that celebrity stylist, so my skills were very green. My timing was slow, and I was becoming a one-trick pony—doing the same highlights on every head of hair. I knew that if I didn't have the skills to back up my marketing, I wouldn't be able to retain these clients.

So, I looked for the best salon in town, where I could learn and grow. It was a big, slick, shiny place with sixteen chairs. Again, because I already had clients, I went to the floor without doing an official apprenticeship, under the condition that I would take some classes with the other apprentices.

The owners loved me because I helped them with their online presence. The salon had been around for twenty years, but this was the early 2000s when having a social media presence became a bigger deal. I helped them start a Twitter page, talked up the importance of this rising social media thing, and helped lead their PR effort.

The downside was that working closely with the owners alienated me from the other stylists. The salon culture was very "us versus them," stylists versus owners, and my peers saw me as being with the owners.

The culture was also cold and full of egos. There were unwritten rules I didn't find out about until after I had broken one. Then I would hear, "Oh, we don't do that here" or "Oh, you can't go behind the reception desk."

I got fired after about a year.

I felt like I had career whiplash going from the small, hands-off salon to the big, flashy one, but neither ended up being a good fit. From those first two experiences, I confirmed what I thought when I started cosmetology school: I don't want to work for someone else. I want to be able to set the tone and the culture. I want to own a salon.

So I started booth renting so I could be my own boss. Booth renting meant I was renting a chair in a salon with other chairs rented by other stylists. The salon provided nothing except the chair. I had to buy my own tools and supplies, wash my own towels at home every night, schedule my own appointments, check each client in and out. I had to figure out my own sick time and reschedule cancellations and do my own taxes as a freelancer.

I worked all the time. I had no manager to blame for being tired or out of product. It was all on me.

In addition, I still had no control over the environment. There was no owner to set salon standards. In the chair next to me, the stylist might be dressed in sweats or talking about her sex life, and I had no say.

While working at a booth rental, I was also planning my wedding. One day I visited my wedding planner at her business site—half of the first floor in a cute little house. The other half was a small boutique. "That would make the cutest salon!" I told her.

"Well, I don't think they're renewing their lease."

And the rest is history. I got married six months later and opened Mirror Mirror the week after my honeymoon.

Thirteen years later, I love my salon and the life it has allowed me to create. But finding a good fit took three-plus years of trial and error, hustle, and grit.

My goal is to save you from a similar three-year ordeal.

The key is finding the right salon from the start, a salon that matches your brand and personality and allows you to thrive. This chapter will help you do just that.

VOICES FROM THE FIELD

I know you're eager to get behind the chair and start doing what you love. Maintain that ambition—but don't let it push you to blow off an apprenticeship. Give yourself time to grow and perfect your skills.

Melanie Hasson, an Educator and Master Colorist in New York, has been in the industry for ten years. She had this to say about her apprenticeship:

> I went right into an apprenticeship, then after a month worked at a blowout bar and really mastered my blowout skills, then after a year went back into apprenticing until I was ready to start building my clientele. That whole process was about three to four years until I was ready to be a full-time stylist.

TYPES OF SALONS

This section may be a refresher for some of you, but don't skip it. Never stop learning, right?

There are two main types of salons: independent and team-based. One is not better than the other. They're just different. It's a matter of how work is scheduled, products are bought, and policies are set. It's also a matter of personal preference and what goes with your personality and work style.

My opinion: it's harder to start off in an independent salon, but I'll let you decide.

INDEPENDENT

In the independent model, you work for yourself. Whether you booth rent, lease a salon suite, or dive right into salon ownership, you are completely on your own. You set your own schedule and prices. You buy your own products and tools. You create your own vibe in your own little space, which may consist of a rented chair next to others who are also creating their own vibe in their own little space.

If you're an ambitious stylist, you are probably hungry to get started. You want to grow fast. And it may seem like the independent path is the way to go. After all, you get to keep all the money you earn, right? If someone pays you a hundred dollars, you get to keep the whole hundred dollars. No one is taking a cut like they do when you work as an employee in a salon.

True, but you're also paying rent and taxes. You're paying for advertising, website hosting, booking software, and fees for professionals like an accountant. You're buying color, shampoo, conditioner, styling products, smocks, capes, clips, combs, brushes, shears, hairdryers, towels, and *everything* else you use as part of your business. You're booking your own headshots, writing your own bios, and likely building your own website.

I've had very senior business-savvy stylists come to Mirror Mirror after working in booth rental because they found being independent was a lot more work for about the same money. Plus, being in a team environment provided camaraderie and support they didn't have on their own. It's a dream for them to walk into a beautiful salon, do beautiful work, and then go home to their families and leave work at work.

Making the leap to the independent model is risky. Never say never, but it's highly unlikely that you will find success in this model right out of school.

Don't take my word for it. Ask stylists you respect. Find out where they started their career. Even if they are successfully independent now, chances are they didn't start out that way.

If you are drawn to the idea of being on your own, look for an apprenticeship under another independent stylist. Many talented stylists working in booth rental or salon suite environments pay out of pocket to have a full-time apprentice. You would not only gain hands-on stylist experience. You would also gain insight into what it's like to be completely on your own.

TEAM-BASED

In the team-based model, you are an employee of a salon. Depending on the salon, you might be paid salary, hourly, or commission, or a combination of salary/hourly and commission.

In the independent model, you can decide when to give yourself a raise. In the team-based model, you typically earn increases in pay as you level up, from apprentice to stylist, and then from new talent to senior stylist and beyond. You might also have benefits like insurance and paid time off.

The team-based model is a lot more turnkey. You don't have to buy your own supplies. You show up with your shears and blow dryer and you're ready to go.

Plus, these salons generally have opportunities for continuing education and training, even after your apprenticeship ends. In this environment, you can learn, grow, and improve. You can shadow more experienced stylists and hone your skills. If you're ambitious and anxious to improve, this might be the perfect place for you.

Even though I started in a team-based salon, I didn't apprentice there. I didn't take the opportunity to learn from others. My attitude was, "I got this. I have clients. I don't need guidance. I just need a place to work."

I now see that this was the wrong approach. I should have apprenticed first.

While the pay ends up being about the same in both models, many stylists ultimately find they crave the support of a team. They like being able to "blame" rate increases and cancellation policies on the salon, while appearing to be the hero to their clients. They like benefits such as health insurance and 401(k) matches. And most importantly, they like being surrounded by like-minded people who see the value of working together, sharing knowledge, and helping out when someone is in a pinch at the shampoo bowl.

Unfortunately, there are plenty of team-based salons with owners who are not involved (remember my first salon?)—salons where you feel like you're on your own even though you're giving them half your earnings. Those are not the salons for you. If you go with the team-based model, you want to work in an environment where leadership actually leads and you feel like they are earning their cut of the commissions.

WHAT TO RESEARCH

In a sense, this is a fork in the road. The rest of the book contains tips and tricks for those taking the team- or commission-based path.

If you're striking out on your own, you won't need to find a salon that fits your vibe, build a résumé, prepare for interviews, or maintain the momentum once you get hired. You are your own boss in every way. Feel free to read along. You may decide team-based is a better fit.

For those of you who want to go into a team-based salon, it's time to start your search for the perfect fit.

ONLINE PRESENCE AND BRAND

It's probably easiest to start with an online search for the best salons in your area. Then visit the websites of those salons.

Team-based salons do not usually advertise as "team-based" or even "commission-based." They might have a section on their website titled "Careers" or "Hiring" where they advertise open positions.

On the other hand, if a salon runs on a booth rental model, they will clearly advertise that. If you see headings like "Available Chair," then you're looking at an independent, booth rental salon as described earlier.

Since you're still in school, why not use a resource that's in front of you every day: your teacher. Ask if she has any recommendations. She might know about salons and apprenticeships that you haven't thought of or that former students have thrived in. Think back to the speakers you had in class. Did any of them talk about their salons? Did any strike you as a good fit?

After you have a list of team-based salons, start digging into their websites and social media feeds. Here are a few areas to focus on:

- **Look for hair pictures.** What kind of work do they do? Does it look interesting to you and match your interests? If you want to specialize in fashion colors but all you see is blonde, that might not be the place for you.
- **Look for pictures of the team.** What are they wearing? Does the style match your own? What can you tell about the personality of the employees? Do they appear playful or more serious?
- **Look for a service and price list.** What services do they offer, and what are they charging for each? Are their "starting at" prices really high? That can be tough when you're getting started and

need a rate that encourages people to give you a shot and also communicates you are a new talent.

- **Look at the website as a whole.** Does it appear outdated? Are there typos? Does it look unprofessional? Attention to detail may not be this salon's strong suit.
- **Look at the name.** Does it contain the owner's name? If so, you might consider why. This isn't a hard-and-fast rule, but owners who put themselves front and center might be more concerned about putting themselves out there than building a strong, cohesive team. Just something to keep in mind.

When you're looking at the online presence of these different salons, your biggest question is: *Do I see myself working there?*

If the answer is no, don't waste your time doing further research. Focus on the salons for which the answer is yes!

SIZE

From the salon's website, you'll probably get a sense of how big the place is, meaning, how many chairs it has. Smaller salons might have six chairs. They probably have a more casual, low-key feel. The rules might be more fluid and the hours more relaxed.

Smaller salons might be newer, which isn't good or bad. It does mean they will probably be ironing out the kinks. You may enjoy being involved in building something, but it likely won't be smooth sailing.

In these smaller environments, there won't be enough room for every stylist to have an apprentice. The owner might only take on one apprentice a year. That means more competition for the available apprenticeships.

At the other extreme, big salons might have twenty chairs. They likely have multiple apprentices at once, so you have your own little cohort learning the ropes together. Tenured, bigger salons tend to be done with growing pains, but they could be stuck in their ways, which can be just as frustrating.

In a bigger salon you'll be exposed to more stylists, more methods and ideas, more possibilities for learning and training. In addition, larger salons can sometimes afford benefits that smaller salons cannot, such as health insurance. That may not be a big deal if you have access to benefits through your parents or a spouse.

Still not sure what size salon is for you? Consider this: if you were planning a birthday party for yourself, would you invite five friends or fifty? If you said five, then you might feel overwhelmed in a salon with thirty or forty stylists. If you said fifty, then you might be bored in a six-chair salon.

Take time to sort out the best fit for you so you can have your own Goldilocks moment and know that you've found the size that's just right.

LOCATION

Another consideration is location. If you live in a big city with plenty of salons, you probably won't have to choose between working where the clients are and working near your home. They'll all be relatively close to each other.

If you live in a smaller town, however, you may not have many options. You may have to choose between driving five minutes to a small salon with no apprenticeship program and commuting forty-five minutes to your dream salon with your dream clients and plenty of growth opportunities.

If you want to learn and grow in your first job, I think it's worth the commute. Some of the stylists at Mirror Mirror drive forty minutes because this is their dream salon: the vibe matches their brand, the salon is centrally located, and we have plenty of call-ins to supplement their own client list. *However*, making this drive for a great apprenticeship with the plan to bounce when you are finished isn't cute.

Again, the question is: *Where do I see myself?* If you don't see yourself sitting in your car for an hour and a half every day, then you either need to move or change your salon choice. If your car is falling apart and it will be at least a year or two before you get a new one, that will also impact your choices, at least for now.

Remember when you were dreaming up hypothetical salons in Chapter 1? Now we're trying to connect the dots between dream and reality. What is the closest version of your dream salon that is also realistic for you in terms of driving time? What sacrifices are you willing to make if you decide to stay close to home?

APPRENTICESHIP PROGRAMS

Cosmetology school is only the beginning of your education as a stylist. It continues in your first salon and beyond.

Don't follow my example here. Learn from my mistakes. Instead of thinking you got this, look for a salon that has an apprenticeship program to help you learn and grow right out of school. My first salon was very small and didn't have apprentices, but the second one did and I could have benefited from that training.

Check the salons' websites to see if they advertise that they are hiring apprentices. Check their social media to see if they post pictures of apprentices working with stylists.

One warning: some salons may use the word *assistant* instead of *apprentice*. In some cases, they mean the same thing: new graduates who are being educated and trained. In some cases, however, they mean *assistant* quite literally: people who sweep the floor, hand the stylist foils, wash hair—and that's it. They're not being trained to have their own chair; they're being used to make other stylists' lives easier.

If you're an ambitious stylist, you'll be miserable in an assistant role.

Don't get me wrong: you'll do some hair-sweeping and towel-folding as an apprentice, just as you will when you're a fully trained stylist. But that shouldn't be your only job. You should be learning to cut and color. You should be learning interpersonal skills. You should be learning how to build and retain a clientele.

As an apprentice, you learn every aspect of the stylist job so you are competent and confident when you are behind the chair.

PICTURE YOURSELF THERE

When I received my certification, I first interviewed at a small boutique salon. I was near accepting the offer, but something made me pause. Fifteen years have passed, and I can't remember exactly what it was—maybe they weren't giving me the schedule I asked for or the culture wasn't resonating with my own values and brand. The bottom line is my gut told me no.

At the last minute, I declined their offer and opted to join the small salon where one of my dearest cosmetology school friends was working. It was also right next door to the Junior League of Austin, a volunteer organization for women that I was involved in. That meant thousands of ideal clients passed the salon every week, which ended up being a tipping point for my career. It catapulted my ability to build a strong clientele early on even though I was only at that salon for a short time. Interestingly, the original salon where I interviewed never really took off. It continued providing meh service for years until it ultimately closed.

Side note: this is exhibit A for why it's so important to make friends in cosmetology school. The classmate I followed to this small salon was twenty years my senior and not someone I would have befriended outside of school. But because we started within a few days of each other and were in the trenches together, we bonded. She was a calm presence in a chaotic environment. She was instrumental in helping me pass my state boards and helped me find this life-changing job.

All of that to say: it pays to practice your people skills in school. Be open. Make friends. It just might change the trajectory of your career!

Deciding where to work after you graduate is a big life decision— especially if you want to make it your home and not a stopping point. Making the move that's right for you requires work and intuition. You have to know yourself. You have to know what you want and where you'll thrive.

To figure that out, you need information. You need to know your options. That's why *the ambitious stylist does her research*.

On those boring days when you're tempted to scroll or bowl mannequin heads or skip school altogether, do some searching. Look at salon websites and social media. Consider the vibe, size, location, and availability of apprenticeship programs. What appeals to you? What turns you off?

Try to picture yourself in each place. Picture yourself being ten minutes from work, walking into a six-chair salon that specializes in highlights and basic cuts, and being the only apprentice. Does that feel right?

How about commuting thirty minutes, working in a twenty-chair salon with a loud rocker vibe, serving clients wearing hair colors from red to green, and being part of an apprentice cohort?

Or how about some combination of these or something in between?

After you have a pretty good idea of what feels right, you can tighten up your search and fill in gaps through informational interviews, which is the first step to getting that dream job.

Journal Challenge

Now is the time to find your dream salon!

1. Google search "Best salon in _____ [your city]." What comes up? Do any of these salons appeal to you? If possible, write down three to five names.
2. Ask your favorite teacher or administrator what salon they picture you in. Don't want to get that specific? Ask them to share what type of salon they picture you in. If possible, write down three to five names.
3. Use social media hashtags to search for salons and stylists in your area (e.g., #austinsalon, #austinhairstylist). Finding stylists in your area that you admire can direct you to your dream salon. If possible, write down three to five salons.

Now look at your three lists. Do any salons pop up on all three? You might be getting closer to finding your dream home!

PART III

Go Get That Job

Chapter 8

INFORMATIONAL INTERVIEWS

DURING MY SENIOR YEAR AT AUBURN UNIVERSITY, I HAD MY EYES set on a big ad agency in Austin with a young, hip vibe. The impressive building was something straight out of a movie set: bright colors, creative conference rooms, foosball tables and bean bag chairs to get the creative juices flowing. This agency had big-time clients like Southwest Airlines, Wal-Mart, and the US Air Force. They created Super Bowl ads and even came up with the now famous phrase "Don't Mess with Texas." It was *the* place to work.

Only one problem: they were on a hiring freeze after 9/11.

I didn't let that deter me. I secured what I call an informational interview with the director of the media department. My goal wasn't to ask for a job. I wanted to find out more about the company and its culture. I also wanted to put myself in a great position for the future. Once the hiring freeze ended and a position opened up, I wanted my name to be top of mind.

Despite our forty-year age difference, the director and I hit it off. Turns out we had been in the same sorority at different universities. I asked her how she got her start and what she loved most about the agency. I asked what she typically looks for in a media planner right out of school. As we talked, I soaked up the vibe: what people were wearing, the smiles on their faces, the fact that they clearly enjoyed working there.

I also asked about the company's core values that were literally carved in stone in the middle of their reception area. *Curiosity* was one of them, which meant "There's always a better way." Years later, I made this value my own at Mirror Mirror, only we used the word *Innovative*.

It was a brief meeting, but I left knowing I wanted to work there. It felt "just right."

My plan worked: seven days before I graduated, I received a call inviting me to come in for an interview.

The University of Texas is in Austin and has one of the top advertising programs in the country. I was in competition with these graduates, many of whom had probably done internships. They were probably more qualified—I had a degree in marketing, not advertising.

But I got the job. Why?

Because I made a good first impression during that informational interview. Otherwise, they would have never heard of me over there in Auburn, Alabama.

For entry-level positions in any industry, the difference maker is not necessarily your skillset. It's your willingness to learn and how you present yourself that will break the tie on résumés.

An informational interview can help you do just that. You let the manager get to know you, while you get to know the manager and the company so everyone is confident this is the perfect match. In this chapter, we'll talk about how to ask for an informational interview, what to say, and what to look for while you're there.

THE GOAL

Plain and simple: an informational interview is an opportunity to gather information. You're not asking for a job or really anything, for that matter. You're gathering information.

Look at your list of dream salons from Chapter 7. Based on your online research, they may seem like a perfect fit: the right distance from home, the right size, the right vibe. You can see yourself working there.

An informational interview gives you a chance to find out if your hunch is correct. You can go into the salon, take a look around, see what kind of clients come in, and watch the stylists at work. All of this information can confirm whether you want to take the next step and apply once you have your license.

An informational interview also helps you practice your people skills. It's a chance to ask the interviewer questions. Find out how they got into the industry and what they love most. People love to talk about themselves. As you listen, you can pick up information about the owner or manager. Can you see yourself working for this person?

How many informational interviews should you do? There's no right or wrong number. Part of it depends on your location and how many salons fit your criteria. Fitting in three to five would be amazing, but that may not be realistic for you. Try to do at least two so you can compare your experiences and findings.

Remember: You're not asking for a job. You're not asking nuts-and-bolts questions about how much they pay, how many apprentices they hire, or their education program. The salon may not even be hiring. That doesn't matter. The goal here is to learn.

THE INTERVIEW

So, how do you go about getting an informational interview? And what do you talk about when you're there? Here are some practical tips for those next steps.

HOW TO ASK

When I asked for a meeting back in 2001, I figured out who the media director was and got her email address. Then I sent a fairly straightforward message introducing myself and telling her why I was writing. I told her I would be in Austin for Thanksgiving (which narrowed down a timeline) and asked if she had fifteen to twenty minutes (which let her know it would be brief) for me to ask her a few questions about her role and the agency in general. Short and sweet. And it worked.

With a salon, I don't recommend calling because the phone is already ringing off the hook. Instead, DM the salon through their social media page. Keep it easy-breezy. Start with a compliment and then present your request. Don't mention anything about looking for a job. You're seeking information. For example:

> Hi! I'm a student at Aveda, and I really admire your salon. I'm trying to learn more about the industry and what it's like working in the salon environment. Would the owner or your manager have fifteen minutes to talk with me?

Warning: if you DM from your Instagram, the salon will check out your social media page before they respond. Guaranteed.

If you've followed the tips in Chapter 6, you're set. If not, I wouldn't DM until you've cleaned up your online presence. Even though you're not asking for a job, you don't want to disqualify yourself before you even get your foot in the door.

If you don't hear back in a week, try messaging the salon through their website. If that doesn't work, put on your cutest, most "on-brand" outfit and pop by the salon to introduce yourself. Or, if you want to try a completely different angle, book a service so you can talk to one of the stylists. (More on that shortly.)

WHAT TO SAY

Congratulations! You secured an informational interview. Now what? You are the one who called the meeting, so you have to be prepared.

Start by thanking the person for her time. Then you might mention something you noticed on their website, something that really caught your attention. You could say something like, "I noticed you guys specialize in extensions" or "It looks like your salon participates in fashion shows" or "I noticed that you all volunteer in the community." This shows you did research before you came in.

Then ask about the person's "why," for example, "Why did you become a stylist? What do you love about your job? What do you love about working here?"

People love telling their stories, and as discussed, it's good for you to hear why others chose this career.

Other possible questions:

- What's the hardest part about your job?
- Does your team hang out together outside of work?
- How long do stylists usually work here?
- [If you're talking to the owner] Are you still behind the chair?
- Do you have apprentices here?
- Did you start out as an apprentice?

Before the interview, write down the questions you want to ask. Then bring the list with you in case your mind goes blank, but don't just read through them one after another. The goal is to engage in conversation. Listen to the answers and respond. Be authentic. If you find an answer interesting, say so. If you haven't thought of the stylist role in the way she describes, say so. This is a great chance to work on those people skills you'll be using every single day when you get your own chair.

If you get stuck, go back to your question list. Pick another "tool" from your toolbelt to make this an interesting, informational dialogue. Ask from a place of curiosity. You're trying to find out if you click with this person. Could you work for her?

The entire interview shouldn't last longer than thirty minutes—unless you are on a roll and the other person seems to be enjoying the conversation. But be respectful of her time. If you told the person fifteen minutes, try to stay close to fifteen minutes.

Chances are that the other person will ask you about yourself. Be ready to answer. You can share where you're from, where you went to college (if applicable), why you're in cosmetology school, and what hobbies you enjoy. As with your online presence, your answers help the person get to know you so she can see if you'd be a good fit down the road.

At the end, ask for advice. You could say something like, "I'm a student, and I'm trying to learn all I can. Do you have any advice for me?"

You might gain some really helpful nuggets. At the very least, asking for advice shows you care about the person's experience and opinion.

You'll hear me say this a few times in this book because it's true: follow-up is key. People are busy and they can unintentionally forget about you. Following up keeps you on their radar.

In addition, following up is an easy way to set yourself apart. As a salon owner who has conducted hundreds of interviews, I can tell you that no one follows up, not even the really good applicants. You will be wildly ahead of your peers if you simply follow up in a genuine way.

Within a few days of your conversation, send a thank-you note. Email is acceptable, but if you send a handwritten note, you'll definitely leave a lasting impression.

Keep the note short and sweet. Start by thanking the person for her time. Then restate something you talked about. This shows you were listening. Finally, compliment the salon in an authentic way. Something you noticed that you really liked.

Note: if you didn't see anything you liked, you don't want to work there. This will probably be the end of your follow-up here. Good thing you went on that informational interview before you applied!

WHAT NOT TO DO

Even though this isn't an official interview, they will be sizing you up. Don't dress too casually. Whatever you saw stylists wearing on the salon website, go 10 percent dressier than that. Show your individual, authentic style, but make sure you're dialing it up a notch. If you study the website and you still don't know what to wear, go with all black.

Also, don't take a résumé, but do take something to write on in case you want to jot down a note or two. You're not asking for a job. You're gathering information.

WHAT TO LOOK FOR

Since you're gaining information about the salon as well as the person you're talking to, make sure you look around and take in the whole scene. You might want to read these questions ahead of time so they're fresh in your mind. Then spend some time reflecting afterward.

- Is the person at the front friendly when you walk in?
- Are the other stylists friendly? Do they make eye contact or completely ignore you?
- What are the stylists wearing? Does it match your brand?
- What are people talking about?
- Are people smiling?
- Do you like the music?
- Do you like the decor?

- How is the lighting?
- Do you like the products they are selling? Are clients buying products as they check out?
- Does the front desk rebook clients?
- Is there excessive hair on the floor?

In addition, take a step back and consider the whole scene: the decor, the music, the attitudes and expressions, the stylists' clothes, hair, and makeup. Does it all match the expectations you developed based on your online research? If someone from this salon visited your school, did she give an impression that is far different from what you see on the floor? In other words, is the salon practicing what it preaches?

As you consider all of these questions, the bottom line is: Does this match your dream? Can you see yourself working in this environment? If not, you've just saved yourself from going through the official interview process. If so, you're ready to take the next step toward making this place your salon home.

Journal Challenge

After each informational interview, pull out your journal and do a gut check: How did you feel when you walked in? How about when you left? Were you excited? Impressed? Unimpressed? Discouraged?

Chances are when you leave, you will have a general feeling about it being a positive or negative experience. Write down any thoughts you have or questions you didn't get answered so you can remember them if you do decide to go back for an actual interview.

BE A SPONGE

Okay. You're at the end of the chapter and you may be thinking, *I don't know if I can do this informational interview thing. It seems so intimidating!* Even though it's not an official interview, it still feels kind of official, right?

How about this: call the salon you're interested in and book a blowout. That gives you one hour in the stylist's chair, which is about three times as long as an informational interview. During that time, you get to observe the stylist on the floor. You get to feel a real service in that dream salon and ask all the questions you want about that stylist: When did they start? What's it like working there?

Don't try to hide the fact that you're a student. If a stylist is rude to a student who is genuinely curious about the industry and the salon, that's a *huge* red flag. That person could be one bad apple, but it could be a comment on the culture as a whole. Definitely something to keep in mind.

Eventually you'll still want to try an informational interview with the manager, but there's no harm in starting with an "informational blowout." Either way, be a sponge while you're there. Absorb everything you can about the salon, the people, the services, the vibe. This is an opportunity to learn more about the industry as well as that specific salon. It gives you early exposure to how salons and other stylists do things. Go in with an open mind, ready to learn. *The ambitious stylist is inquisitive, curious, and genuine.*

If you think you'll blank and forget your possible questions, write them in your phone. Better to look down at your list than to sit there silent. You're the one who initiated this meeting, so do what's necessary to be ready.

These informational interviews set you up for the next stage of your job search: résumé building.

VOICES FROM THE FIELD

Chelle Neff, Founder and CEO of Urban Betty, has been in the industry for thirty years. Here's some advice she wishes someone would have shared with her early on:

Let me share something I wish I had known when I was starting out. First, steer clear of any salon or company that tries to tie you down with noncompete agreements. Your talent deserves to shine without any limitations holding you back.

Here's a secret I've learned: in the salon world, there's no such thing as competition in the traditional sense. Imagine a pie, and each of us has our slice. Your success doesn't take away from mine, and vice versa. We're all in this together, building our own pies side by side. When I win, you win.

So, when looking for a place to kickstart your career, find a salon that cheers you on as you grow. Surround yourself with people who are all about lifting each other up, not tearing each other down. Trust me, it makes all the difference.

In this field, your creativity is your currency, and the more you surround yourself with fellow creatives, the richer you'll become. So go ahead, chase your dreams, find your tribe, and get ready to make your mark in the world of hair.

Chapter 9

RÉSUMÉ BUILDING

IF YOU GOOGLE "HOW TO WRITE A RÉSUMÉ," YOU WILL MOST likely get tips geared toward corporate jobs. They'll say things like, "Don't include a photo" and "Use a business template" because that's the standard for the corporate world.

Salons are not corporate. We're a service industry. We want to get to know you. Include that photo. Share your hobbies. Tell us about your dog-sitting experience.

Ninety percent of the résumés I see miss this point. I can tell which applicants went online, looked up "how to write a résumé," found a template, and simply filled in the blanks. The result is something that works if you are applying for a job at a dentist's office or bank, but not a salon like Mirror Mirror.

In a sense, the word *résumé* is almost too formal for what you're sending to a potential employer. Think of it as a snapshot: a one-sheet picture of you—your personal brand, style, and personality—as well as your experience.

In this chapter, we'll discuss tips for building a targeted, attractive, and informative snapshot. A snapshot for one specific job at one specific salon. A snapshot that offers just the right amount of information—enough to pique the person's interest enough to invite you in for the interview.

Ready to learn?

HOW TO CREATE A SNAPSHOT

We work in a fashion-forward industry, which means things move at light speed. I don't want to offer specific tips that will be irrelevant six months from now. I do want to empower you to do some research.

So, I'm offering general guidelines in résumé, or snapshot, building that you can adapt and update as needed.

TEMPLATES

From my earlier comments, you might think I'm against using generic résumé-building templates. Not at all.

Resources like Canva, Etsy, or even Google can be quite helpful for creating complete, aesthetically pleasing résumés, especially for those of us who are not graphic artists. Pinterest is also full of great inspiration, and if you want to keep it really simple, Microsoft Word will get it done with the right formatting and a crisp font.

That said, don't get locked into the number of preset slots for past job experience, education, or special skills. Be comfortable adjusting the template so that it fits you, your style, and the service-industry job you're seeking.

No matter what template you use, here's one must: *keep it to one page*. Managers are busy people. Help them grab a snapshot of you without turning the page. More pages also means more potential printing problems. Plus, the second page is never as cute as the first, is it? If you're going from cosmetology school to the salon, you're applying for an entry-level position, so keep it simple. Even if you've been in the workforce and have a ton of previous experience, it's unlikely that all of that experience is relevant to the new career you are venturing into. So, remember the mantra: one page.

KEY ELEMENTS

Statistics show that recruiters spend an average of six to eight seconds reviewing a résumé. That's why you need a clean, simple, one-page snapshot. The person reviewing your résumé should be able to glance at it and easily see your photo, skills, experience, and education.

There's no right or wrong way to organize the following sections. The important part is to have them clearly labeled and keep them on one page.

Photo

Including a photo might feel cringy and awkward, especially if you've submitted résumés for jobs in other industries where photos are a big no-no. I get it. I had the same reaction when I applied for my first salon job. The owner of my cosmetology school insisted I include a photo. That went against everything I had been taught. But she was adamant. "You need to present yourself. This is an aesthetic industry."

The owner was right. I included a photo when I applied for my first two jobs, and I got both. I've been sharing this tip ever since.

You do need to use a certain kind of photo—something professional, not from the day you went to the beach. Also, the person in the photo on your résumé should match the person who walks into the interview. We all love a photoshopped blemish, but don't get carried away. You don't want to end up looking like a Disney princess.

Another tip: lay off the filters. You want your photo to look as natural and as close to your real-life likeness as possible.

All of that said—you don't have to include a photo. I've hired some talented stylists who submitted a clean, clearly formatted résumé with no photo. If you don't have a professional-looking shot, better to focus on the overall formatting and leave out the pic. Plus, if you followed my tips, your social media has excellent photos, and the employer can check you out there too.

Contact Info

Your contact info should at least include your name, phone number, email address, and social media handle. Including your address or city and state is optional.

Statistics show that three in ten résumés are rejected because they have an unprofessional email address. There's no excuse for having an unprofessional email address. Email addresses are free. You can create one right now in a few minutes.

Professional means your name or your name and a number, for example, FirstLast23@gmail.com. By *unprofessional* I mean something like 2003GlitterGal, UrGirlCharleen, or ABoyWithDreams (yes, these are all real examples!).

About Me

This section is a brief opportunity to tell your future employer about yourself. If you include a cover letter or email with your résumé, you can pull a few highlights from the About Me section to include in that letter/email.

I reviewed the résumés of apprentices I've hired and identified the About Me facts that stood out to me:

- **Geography:** Where you live or where you're from, for example, "Originally from Alabama. I have lived in Austin for 8 years." "Born and raised in Austin."
- **Your "why":** A one- to two-sentence version of the "why" you came up with in Chapter 1. Make sure it includes something that tugs on the reader's emotions, for example, "I've always loved hair and makeup." "My grandmother was a cosmetologist." "I love making people feel good about themselves."
- **Hobbies/interests:** Something you enjoy outside of school and the industry. Remember: you're helping the manager get to know you. Some examples: "When I'm not in school I love _____ [trying new restaurants, trail running, watching Bravo, shopping,

photography]." You can leave out "I love going to the bar every night of the week."

- **Excitement for the job or industry:** Something specific to the salon or the job, for example, "I am thrilled to finally pursue my dream of being a hairstylist." "I am really passionate about blonding and extensions and can't wait to further my education." "I love that you and your team volunteer for Habitat for Humanity and look forward to hearing more about it." "I am so excited to continue my education and contribute to a salon in a meaningful way."

Make sure your answers are sincere and authentically you.

Skills

Don't feel like you have to list every skill you've learned in every job you've had since you were thirteen. Remember our mantra: one page.

Pick the skills that seem most relevant to the work you'll be doing as a stylist. Abilities like multitasking and customer service are the most obvious, but think outside the box: for example, knowing CPR and being bilingual could definitely come in handy in a service industry.

Let's do a reality check using the skills list I received from a real applicant named "Anna." Look at the organization of the list as well as the items themselves:

- Speak/translate Spanish
- Multitasking
- Organizing
- Dependable
- Responsible
- Server
- Organizational Skills
- Customer Service

- PowerPoint
- Typing
- Front Desk
- Microsoft Word
- Microsoft Excel
- English
- Photography
- Computer skills
- Sales
- Microsoft Office
- Help desk
- Business development
- Adobe Lightroom

What do you think? What would you have eliminated or done differently?

Here are a few observations as an owner/interviewer:

1. The organization shows a lack of attention to detail, like Anna brainstormed a list and then didn't go back to review it. Example: (Microsoft) PowerPoint is listed ninth, followed by two unrelated skills, followed by Microsoft Word and Microsoft Excel, followed by four unrelated skills and then Microsoft Office. Why not list them all together? Why list the individual programs as well as Microsoft Office?

2. Knowing English should be a given if you're applying for a job in the United States. No need for Anna to mention it, especially since her résumé was three pages long—and written in English. This is something she could have cut.

3. Words like *dependable* and *responsible* are so similar. Keep an eye out for redundancy.

By contrast, here's a skills list that appeared on another applicant's résumé:

- Extensions
- Lived-in color
- Blonding
- Social media marketing
- Content editing
- Photography
- Retail sales

"Grace" kept her list short and sweet, and she included a combination of stylist-specific and more general skills. I love that she included photography, for example, because it shows that she is artistic and most likely knows how to use social media.

There's no one set list of skills that should be included. You need to think about the salon, the position, and your experience, and create a list that shows you're a perfect match.

Certifications

Many schools give certifications in specific classes. If this is the case at your school, list the different certifications you've received. Some examples include:

- Hydrafacials
- Chemical peels
- Lash extensions
- Lash/brow tinting
- Advanced razor cutting
- Editorial styling
- Makeup
- Full-body waxing

If you have a ton, you don't have to list them all. A few relevant ones will show that you went above and beyond in school. That said, if I had to choose between a long list of certifications with no work experience and no certifications with experience in retail and restaurants, customer service wins!

Experience

Salons are looking for ambitious stylists, people who are organized, disciplined, and self-motivated. People who don't need to be babysat. Whatever your previous work experience, you can use your résumé to show you've got what it takes to succeed.

List your work experience in reverse chronological order, with the most recent job first. Be sure to include your job title, dates employed, and the name of the company, as well as your responsibilities.

You don't have to list every job you've ever had. Remember, you only have one page. Pick the jobs that have the greatest relevance to the work you'll be doing as a stylist: jobs involving customer service (retail), multitasking (retail, restaurants), and responsibility (babysitting, working in a preschool or day camp).

Look for ways to elevate job titles that are not specifically salon-related. For example, instead of *babysitter*, say that you were a *nanny*. If you worked in the beauty department at a store like Target, you could call yourself a *beauty consultant*. Don't lie, but do put your position in the best light using elevated language. Also, highlight the job title first, rather than the store or restaurant. People may not have heard of the business, so don't lead with that.

Having gaps in your résumé is fine; just be ready to talk about why. Did you attend college on a soccer scholarship, so you didn't have time to work? Did you take a few years off when your kids were young?

If you're in school, you likely won't have a prior stylist job, but that's okay. If you've worked any kind of customer service job—food service, bartending, hotels, boutiques, for example—you have valuable experience working with people under pressure. If you've worked as a preschool teacher or nanny, that shows you're trustworthy and responsible. Positions in law offices, accounting firms, and doctors' offices also show you are trustworthy since you regularly handle sensitive information.

Employers are looking for people who have stuck with a job for a while. If you've worked three months here and three months there, why should the owner think you're going to stay longer than three months if she hires you?

If your history shows three months here and there, you'll need to reassure the person that this pattern is changing. You could use your About Me section to explain that you have spent the last few years finding your place. Cosmetology school has given you the direction you were seeking. You're ready to settle into a job.

Even if you say that you're changing, your dream salon may not be willing to roll the dice on you. You may need to work for a year or more at your second choice to show that you can hold a job for more than three months. That's the deal.

I love it when an applicant has receptionist or front desk experience, especially if that experience was at a hair salon. The sooner you can get into the salon environment in some capacity, the better. It's not required, but it's a nice bonus that might set you apart.

If your résumé shows you are currently working, that's a good thing. That means you are holding down a job while going to school, which shows you are able to manage your time.

If you list everything and your work experience still looks thin, think of extracurricular activities that required hard work, discipline, commitment, punctuality, and ambition—for example, sports teams, cheerleading, student body leadership, club leadership, and volunteer work. Even if you haven't held a paying job, your résumé needs to show how you have been filling your time.

Personal Stats and Achievements

Many cosmetology schools hand out awards for Student of the Month, Best Attendance, and more. If you receive one or more of these awards, be sure to include them on your résumé. High attendance in particular looks good because it tells the employer that you show up. It's another sign that you have discipline.

Your school might also track metrics like retail sales or prebooking or treatment sales. If so, find out what your metric is in each category and add it to your résumé.

In addition, you can start your own list of achievements, for example, number of clients served, attendance record, and any monthly awards given by the school. The very fact that you kept track of your stats shows ambition.

Education

If you're straight out of high school, then that will likely be the only education for you to list, besides cosmetology school. If you went to college before cosmetology school, list that as well along with your major and graduation year.

Journal Challenge

Now that you have the details that go into a résumé, start brainstorming what will go in yours. Make a list of the sections mentioned earlier and then make a quick list of what you could say in each section. Then evaluate what you have and ask yourself:

- Do I need to work on some areas? Which ones?
- Do I have way too much in some areas? What is the most important to include? (Remember: one page!)

Another task: start looking for a résumé template and for photos that might be appropriate. If you can't find a pic, you have plenty of time to have someone take one.

FONTS AND COLORS

Use the formatting of your résumé to highlight your personal brand—a brand that should match the salon where you're applying. For example, if your style is more masculine and the salon has a similar minimalist vibe, your résumé should not have an ornate, script-like font with pink text boxes. You'd be better off with earth tones and a simple font.

A few general tips on font and color:

- A script-like font is fine for your name if it fits your aesthetic, but it's not a good choice for headings or the main text. Keep the main font simple, clean, and easy to read.
- In terms of font color, black is probably your best bet.
- Using all caps, LIKE THIS, is fine for headings, but not for the main text. It feels like you're shouting at the person reading.

After you design your template, save the document as a PDF. That will "lock" in what you've done. PDF is also a standard format for a document you attach to an application or email.

After you save the file, print it off in black and white to make sure it's still legible. Colored text boxes look great on screen, but they don't always translate well to the printed page. Most potential employers will print your résumé before the interview. You want the page to be easy to read.

Additional reasons for printing it out:

- To make sure all of the text stays on one page.
- To make sure you don't have blank pages at the end. Sometimes the document will look like one page onscreen, but when printed, you'll have a stray line on page two.

After your résumé is printed, have at least one person read it. The more the merrier. Have them look for typos, misspelled words, dropped letters, errors in capitalization, and so on.

Better to have your friend find those mistakes than the salon owner.

SEND IT OFF

After you've printed your résumé, proofread it, made corrections, and printed it out again just in case, you're ready to send it off.

The best time to apply for an apprenticeship is one to three months before graduation. Check the salon's website for a place to apply. Usually there will be a place to attach your résumé and write a short message. If you can't find a place to apply online, look for an email on the Contact Us page.

When you send your résumé, include a cover letter or at the very least an email that introduces who you are. If you've written an About Me section in your résumé, you can keep this intro very brief—just a couple of sentences that communicate (1) why you went to cosmetology school and why being a stylist is appealing (tip: your answer should probably include some variation on loving customer service, helping others, making people happy) and (2) what makes you a perfect fit for that salon (e.g., comment on the salon's aesthetic or Instagram page. Show that you've done your research. Be genuine.)

If you're applying for an apprenticeship, also emphasize your desire to continue learning, growing, and pushing yourself.

If you can't find a place to submit your résumé electronically, consider driving to the salon to drop off your résumé in person. Print your cover letter and your résumé on nice cardstock, dress up in a cute outfit, and drive on over. *The ambitious stylist figures out a way to make herself seen by her dream salon.*

THREE QUESTIONS

Salon owners, this one's for you.

As you may already know, many students don't know how to write a cover letter. (Psst, students: if you're ambitious, you'll learn to do this and set yourself apart!) So I ask three basic questions as part of the initial application:

1. Tell us about yourself.
2. Tell us a little bit about your past work experience and why you want to join the team.
3. Tell us anything else that makes you the right fit for Mirror Mirror.

The answers should have gone in a proper cover letter. This is my way of pulling the answers out of them to give them a second shot.

SECURING REFERENCES: DOS AND DON'TS

A separate part of résumé building is securing references—people who will vouch for you, your character, and your work skills. Try to get one reference in three different categories:

- **A cosmetology school reference:** a teacher who can speak to your attitude, skills, and attendance
- **A professional reference:** a boss who can speak to the responsibility, discipline, customer service, and other skills you displayed in that job; preferably from your most recent relevant job
- **A personal reference:** a nonparent adult who can speak to your personality and character

In each case, think of people who will speak highly of you. Know yourself and how you've acted around these people. If you have any doubts at all about what they would say, don't ask them to be a reference. Find someone else.

Before you give the salon their names, ask the people if you can put them down as a reference. And before you start asking, make sure you've finished your résumé. Some may ask to see your résumé to give them ideas for talking points.

Whether you ask in person or over the phone depends on the relationship. If you're still in school and you see your teacher every day, then asking in person makes sense. If you ask a high school track coach but you no longer live in your hometown, then you may need to call, email, or text.

However you ask, keep it short and sweet. You could say something like, "I'm nearing the end of cosmetology school [you can omit that part with your cosmetology school teacher], and I'm starting to apply for jobs. I would love to use you as a reference. Would that be okay? I'm happy to give you a copy of my résumé so you have it in case they call."

If they say yes, be gracious and say thank you. And if they ask for a résumé, be sure to supply it.

KEEP IT SIMPLE

How are you feeling about writing your résumé? Are you worried about making it ultra cute so you stand out and get hired?

Let that go.

Some of the best apprentices at Mirror Mirror used a basic template with a clean font. Nothing fancy. One even used Microsoft Word. Focus on including the necessary information in a simple, one-page format. Print it out to make sure it's all on one page. Have someone proofread it. And then send it off. You got this!

With a crisp, polished résumé, you are more likely to pique the interest of a potential salon. Next step: nailing the interview.

Chapter 10

THE INTERVIEW

WHEN "CHRISSY" CAME INTO THE INTERVIEW, SHE WAS READY to talk. But she was disorganized and couldn't keep her thoughts straight. She also kept interrupting me, which is a big no-no in an interview.

Somewhere in the midst of her rambling, Chrissy said, "I wanna be a salon owner someday, so I really wanna just come in and learn from you so that I can do that, and I'm interviewing at another salon and she's willing to mentor me and teach me how to be a salon owner."

Then she switched topics and started talking about something completely unrelated.

Then she started crying. "Oh my gosh. I can't believe I'm crying in an interview."

"Oh, that's okay," I said, trying to make her feel better. "People cry in here sometimes."

"Well, that's *weird,*" Chrissy blurted out.

It was one of the strangest interviews I've ever held.

Chrissy may have been extremely nervous. That's a natural

response when you're being interviewed by the owner for a job you really, really want.

Still, you can't interrupt your interviewer; that demonstrates a lack of people skills. You also can't start talking about salon owner-ship when you haven't even been an apprentice. It sounds ambitious, but think about it from the owner's perspective: why would she pour time, energy, and money into training you, knowing from the start that you're not going to stay?

If you've been following the tips provided so far, you're already better prepared. You know yourself and your ideal salon. You've identified your brand and cleaned up your online presence. You've had at least one informational interview where you got some of that nervousness out of your system. Now I'll provide you with a prepara-tion timeline, as well as questions to ask during the interview itself.

With these tools, you can walk into each interview in a calm, confident headspace and show that you belong.

PREPARATION TIMELINE

Everything we've talked about so far is leading up to this stage: interviewing for and hopefully getting your first job. No pressure, but it's go time!

I want to help you be as prepared as possible, so I've broken down your tasks into four timeframes. If you follow this timeline, you won't be cramming it all in at the last minute. You'll be ready.

Note: this is a general timeline. You may be reading this less than a month from your interview. Don't panic! You can knock out all of the following fairly quickly.

ARE YOU READY?

Time for another reality check: Have you started working on the tasks from Chapters 1–8? Have you identified your dream salon? Have you cleaned up your online presence?

If not, there's no sense in preparing for a job interview. You're not ready.

That may sound harsh, but it's true. You need to know what kind of stylist you want to be and where you want to work before you prepare a résumé that targets that salon, let alone go to an actual interview.

If you're not ready, that's okay. Now's the time to get there. You can start working on most of these items from day one in cosmetology school:

- You know why you want to be a stylist.
- You know what kind of stylist you want to be.
- You know what kind of salon you want to work in.
- You've created a List of Twenty.
- You've started networking and building your clientele.
- You've started inviting people in for blowouts.
- You've identified your personal brand and started making conscious choices to showcase it.
- You've cleaned up your online presence.
- You have a short list of ideal salons.
- You've started asking for informational interviews.

After you've checked off the above, move on to the One Month Before Graduation checklist.

ONE MONTH BEFORE GRADUATION

One month before graduation you should be doing some prep work: verifying facts, gathering data, writing your résumé, and so on. We talked about many of these things in the last chapter.

- **Check your hours:** Make sure you know how many hours you need to graduate and how many hours you currently have.
- **Pass the written exam:** Check your school's policy, but most allow you to take the written when you're within one hundred hours of graduation. Also check the guidelines about retaking the written part, just in case.
- **Gather stats and achievements:** Whether you ask your teacher or find the information yourself, it's time to locate your awards and achievements related to attendance, sales, number of clients, and more.
- **Prepare your résumé:** Write your résumé, print it out, have someone else read it, and revise it as necessary.
- **Secure your references:** Ask your teacher, boss, and nonparent adult if they will write a letter of recommendation.
- **Start applying for jobs:** Check your dream salon's website. Are they hiring? Time to get your résumé into their hands. The truth is, most salons are always hiring and would never turn down an excellent candidate. Even if your dream salon doesn't advertise an open position, send your cover letter and résumé anyway!

In that last month before graduation, there's a lot going on. You're working hard to get all of your hours. You're looking forward to being done. You're excited about starting an apprenticeship. That's all good. Be excited! Just don't get senioritis. You've got to keep your foot on the gas all the way to the end—and beyond!

Congratulations! You graduated—or you're really close. You applied for a job and got invited in for an interview. That's something to celebrate.

Now your interview is one week away. What should you be doing to prepare?

- **Know your answers to common questions:** You can't prepare for every question, but there are a few common ones. Know how you'll answer the following:
  - Why did you go to cosmetology school?
  - Why did you choose our salon?
  - Where do you see yourself three to five years from now?
  - What are you looking for in an ideal salon home?
  - Tell us about your role at _____ [an employer on your résumé].
  - Are there any specific scheduling restraints we should know about?
  - What do you love most about doing hair?
  - What do you enjoy doing outside of school?

    That last one tells the owner more than what your hobbies are. It shows her that you have a life outside of the salon where you will continue networking and building a clientele.
- **Do research on the salon:** Start combing the salon's website so you can comment on something that resonates. Write down your thoughts and bring them with you just in case you go blank.
- **Think about what you'll wear:** Remember: this isn't corporate. You're interviewing for the vibe. If you've followed the tips given so far, you've picked a salon with an aesthetic and style that match your own. That means you should have appropriate clothing to wear. However, you do want to kick it up a notch—add about 10 percent extra to your basic style. It's better to overshoot formality than show up dressed too casually. By starting

a week early, you have time to buy something if what you have doesn't work.

- **Get your hair cut and colored as needed:** This one should be self-explanatory. Your hair must look good. In general, start to mentally prepare and be aware of your calendar so you aren't feeling burned-out heading into the interview!

ONE DAY BEFORE THE INTERVIEW

Remember Chrissy? The best word to describe the way she came across during the interview is *chaotic*. She jumped around from topic to topic and talked a mile a minute. I couldn't follow her train of thought.

Don't be like Chrissy.

The day before your interview, you need to take intentional steps to prepare and calm yourself so you can answer questions in a clear, nonchaotic way.

This checklist may feel like overkill, but you've come so far. Don't leave anything to chance. *The ambitious stylist does everything she can to stack the cards in her favor.*

- **Set aside time to be quiet:** You may not have a whole day, but at least set aside an hour or two to center yourself—whatever that looks like for you. You could get a massage, take a nap, read a good book, or get your nails done (definitely get a manicure if your nails are chipped; see below). Put yourself in a calm, unfrazzled state of mind.
- **Confirm your appointment:** Want to make a good impression before you even start the interview? Email or call the point person to let her know you're looking forward to your appointment. A simple, one-line message will work: "Hi, So and So. I'm looking forward to our meeting tomorrow at 10 a.m. Can't wait to see you guys."
- **Print your résumé:** You should have already confirmed that your

résumé fits on one page and that it looks good in black and white. Print out a few copies on nice paper and bring them with you.

- **Make sure your nails are clean and not distracting:** That might mean you need a manicure to fix chips and tone down the wild color. The salon may be fine with hot pink and electric green one-inch nails, but for the interview, play it safe. You don't want people to be distracted. At the very least, make sure your nails are trimmed and clean.

- **Do a dress rehearsal:** There is nothing worse than thinking something is clean and ready, and it's not. Or trying on the new top and skirt, and discovering they don't pull together as you thought. Or finding out those cute pants no longer fit. After you make sure everything looks exactly how you want it to look, leave the outfit out so it's ready to go the next day.

- **Put gas in your car and map out your route:** The day before, make sure your car has gas, make sure you know where you're going, and make sure you know how long it takes to get there at the time of day you're driving. Then add fifteen minutes to the estimated time, just in case. It's better to arrive thirty minutes early and sit in a nearby coffee shop than to run in breathless at the last minute or, worse, five minutes late. You cannot be late for an interview. If you are, you might as well turn around and drive back home.

- **Review your notes:** Last week, you prepared answers to common questions and took notes on the salon's website. Now's the time to review those notes. Practice talking out loud. Maybe even have a friend ask you a few questions so you can practice responding to another human.

- **Choose questions to ask the interviewers:** At the end of the interview, you will most likely be asked what questions you have. Be ready! If you don't have anything when they ask, "What questions do you have for me?" the interview is likely over. That doesn't mean you won't get the job, but the more time you can spend with the key decision-makers, the more likely you are to secure the position. Look at the list of questions included in this chapter and choose five that stand out to you. Pick the ones that feel the most natural flowing out of your mouth. If you get awkward or frantic asking about compensation, then don't ask that question. Write down your five and take them with you.

- **Set everything out:** You already laid out your outfit. Do the same with your water, purse, car keys, and copies of your résumé. Anything you want to take with you should be out and ready to go so you're not running around like crazy the next day.
- **Get some rest:** This is not the night to go out partying. It's too risky. You don't want to wake up hungover or sick. Save it for a celebration after you get your dream job!

If all goes well during this interview, you could be offered a position at your dream job. That prospect is probably exciting and overwhelming. You might still *feel* nervous when you walk in, but if you prepare, you won't come off as frantic and chaotic.

QUESTIONS TO ASK THE INTERVIEWER

Here's a list of possible questions to ask when it's your turn. **Don't feel like you have to ask all of them. Pick five that stand out to you and write them down.** When the time comes, ask two or three from your list that haven't been answered in what they've already said.

Where it may not be immediately obvious, I added a comment to indicate what the interviewer's answer can tell you about the salon.

Questions about the Nitty-Gritty Stuff

- **When are you looking to fill the position?**
- **Do you have set times for breaks, or do stylists take breaks as they can during processing times?** Whether you are a "I must

have an hour to go out to lunch everyday" kind of girl or someone who feels like having an official lunch break messes up your scheduling, you'll want to get that info during the interview.

- **What is your dress code?**

Questions about the Salon/Team

- **Would it be possible to meet with a few of your stylists or shadow for a bit so I can get a feel for the flow of the salon?** If the answer is no, that could be a big red flag. What are they hiding? On the other hand, it could mean they're really busy. Consider their answer in conjunction with the other info you gather.
- **What do you love about your job?** If someone is genuinely happy with their job, they will light up when they talk about it. Their response should roll off the tongue. If they pause or have to really think about it, that could be a red flag.
- **How do you handle call-ins?** Some salons give call-ins to the stylists with the highest prebooking percentage or retail sales. Other salons assign call-ins randomly. It's just good information to have up front.
- **Do you have team-building activities? How often?** This just tells you a little about the salon culture.
- **How many of your former apprentices still work here as stylists?** If apprentices are going through the program and then sticking around, that means the salon is setting them up for success. If the salon is more of an apprentice factory, pumping out stylists who go work elsewhere, think twice about moving forward. You might be better off seeking out another salon where apprentices are trained and retained.

Questions about the Business Side

- **What kind of revenue does a new stylist generate?** This shows the interviewer is aware of their numbers, as they should be.

- **What is your prebooking percentage?** To me, a high prebooking percentage shows retention and customer loyalty, but a salon with a lot of walk-ins could be equally busy but not have a high percentage.
- **What is your productivity percentage?** Asking about productivity and prebooking shows the owner that you are aware of the metrics that make a salon successful. Like prebooking, a high productivity percentage shows customer loyalty. It also shows that stylists are making the most of their time, which means bigger paychecks.
- **(If the salon seems *really* quiet, ask) It seems so quiet. Is this normal?** A dead salon might be a reason to run for the hills, or it might mean you came between shifts.
- **How are apprentices compensated? How about stylists?**
- **What does your typical junior stylist make in their first year on the floor?**
- **What does your average stylist make?**
- **How do you market your business for new stylists?** When you are new, it's helpful to know up front if you will be on your own to build a clientele, or if the salon invests in search engine optimization, digital marketing, and/or traditional advertising to help stylists gain clients.

Questions about Your Role There

- **If an apprentice has a clientele, on average how long does it take to get on the floor?** Use this wording, rather than "How long is the apprenticeship program?" or "How long until I get on the floor?" You don't want to communicate that you're rushing or that you think you don't have much to learn.
- **I already have clients I've been servicing during cosmetology school. How do you handle that?** If you can't start seeing your own clients until you finish the year apprenticeship, then you're

going to be playing kitchen beautician on Sundays to handle your customers. You're setting yourself up for exhaustion.

- **How do you handle continuing education?** If they do offer continuing education, ask if they provide time off to attend. If they don't, you might have to use vacation days.
- **What does a typical day look like for an apprentice?**
- **How closely does the leadership/management work with the apprentices?** It might be a red flag if the leadership has no interaction with the apprentices at all. I'm not in the trenches on the floor, but I still mentor and coach all of our apprentices.

In addition to these questions, feel free to ask others that come to you during the interview. Your list of five will still be there if you get stuck.

The moral of the story is this: the answer to the question, "Do you have any questions for me?" is never "No" or "You covered everything."

An ambitious stylist wants to know more.

DAY OF THE INTERVIEW

The big day! If you prepared the day before, today should be a breeze.

- **Rise and shine with plenty of time:** Give yourself extra time to get ready and drive to the interview. Think about the time you'll need to do all the things—showering, dressing, styling your hair, putting on makeup and jewelry, driving—and then add a buffer of at least thirty minutes.
- **Don't smoke or vape:** If you are a smoker, lay off before your interview. You don't want the smell following you into the salon.
- **Arrive fifteen minutes early and be present:** The interviewer

likely won't meet with you right away. You may be tempted to get on your phone. Don't do it! Stay present. Be friendly and confident with the front desk team. Make eye contact and smile at everyone you see. Look around. Is the salon clean? Do the stylists and guests appear happy? Is their work impressive? Are guests rebooking when they check out? Listen to the conversations going on around you. If you did an informational interview at this salon, this is a good chance to confirm your first impressions are accurate.

- **Greet interviewers by name with a firm handshake:** If you've never been taught how to properly shake hands, go ask someone to teach you. If the interviewers are like me, they will not be impressed by a wet-noodle grip. As you shake hands, greet the person by name and then offer a genuine compliment. For example, "It's nice to meet you, _____ [insert name]. Thank you so much for having me. This is a beautiful salon." Or "It's nice to meet you, _____ [insert name]. Thank you so much for having me. Everyone seems so happy." If you can't think of one genuine compliment, this probably isn't the place for you.

- **Mirror their body language:** After you take a seat, take note of how the interviewers are sitting. Are they leaning forward? Are they sitting back with one leg crossed over the other? Try to mirror their body language. Research shows mirroring can make the other person more willing to open up. It also shows you are attentive and interested in what the interviewer has to say.

- **Let them take the lead:** Now they will start asking questions. Don't worry! You're prepared. And you're not expected to know everything about everything. If you don't have an immediate answer, don't get flustered. Simply say something like, "That's a great question. Let me think for a second." Then respond. If you truly don't know the answer, say something like, "That's a great question. I may have to get back to you later." The way you respond is as important as the answer itself, so it's important to stay calm.

- **Ask your questions:** Here's where you'll need your list of questions. Depending on what you've already learned, you may ask two or three from your list of five. Remember: ask the ones that flow most naturally so you don't get tongue-tied.

- **End with a thank-you and compliment:** After you ask your questions, the interview will most likely come to an end. Thank the interviewers for their time and repeat something specific that came out during your discussion. For example, "Thank you for your time. I am excited about this opportunity. I really love how you handle celebrations here. It is so thoughtful." Then ask when you should follow up and let them know that you are looking forward to hearing from them. If it's true, you can also let them know that you are interviewing elsewhere. Nothing gets me moving faster than when a good candidate tells me they're interviewing elsewhere.

- **Walk out with a smile:** When the interview ends, walk out with the same positive energy you brought in. Smile at people on the way out. Compliment a stylist if you notice she's doing an excellent blowout. Thank the person at the front desk. Leave everyone with a good impression.

Congratulations! Give yourself a big high five and take yourself out for your favorite beverage. You just completed a huge milestone.

But don't get too comfortable. There's one key step in the interview process that most people neglect: follow-up.

FOLLOW-UP TIMELINE

If you've been following the tips since Chapter 1, you've already set yourself apart as a candidate for that job. If you put a little effort into follow-up, you will likely seal the deal. And it starts within a few hours of finishing the interview.

WITHIN A FEW HOURS

Your first step is easy: pull out your phone and send a short thank-you note via email. You can go old school if you want and send a handwritten note, but email is perfectly fine in today's world.

Here's a fill-in-the-blank template you can use for this note:

Good morning!

Thank you for your time. I really enjoyed _____ [fill in something specific you talked about] from our conversation. I can absolutely see myself contributing and thriving at XYZ Salon.

If you have any additional questions, please don't hesitate to reach out.

Thank you again for your time. I look forward to hearing from you.

WITHIN A FEW DAYS

You have a few follow-up tasks in the days following your interview. Don't take your foot off the gas just yet.

Reflect

Over the next few days, take time to reflect on your interview. Don't wait a week or more. Reflect while the experience is fresh in your mind.

Think about the whole experience, from the time you walked in until the time you left—conversations, observations, thoughts, feelings, hunches. Did what you see and hear align with your values? Did people treat others in a way that mirrors your brand? Did you get a sense of the culture? Does it match your desired work environment?

Comb through the experience looking for the standout moments, positive or negative. Was there a point when you got goosebumps and/or thought, *I've found my salon home for life!* For me, it was different at each salon. The first small salon gave me a sense of comfort and belonging. At the second salon, the larger environment and upscale aesthetic gave me a sense of excitement and just enough intimidation to make me want to push myself harder.

Or did a comment or observation leave you wanting to run for the hills? For me, positivity and mutual respect are nonnegotiables. I don't tolerate gossip or negativity. If the interviewer started speaking negatively about the business or a stylist, I would try to wrap up that interview and move on.

People are supposedly on their best behavior in an interview. If someone gossips or is rude to another employee in that setting, you can expect it to be even worse on a normal workday when their guard is down. That's just human nature.

Journal Challenge

To help you reflect, pull out your journal and answer the following questions:

- What do you think went well?
- Did you stumble over a certain question? How would you answer it next time?
- Is there a question you wish you would have asked?
- What did you like about the salon environment? What did you dislike?
- Did you have a "goosebumps moment"?
- Did you at any point want to run for the hills? Did a comment or observation make you question whether the salon is the place for you?
- Can you see yourself working there?

When you're fresh out of school and interviewing for your first job, it's easy to get blinded by the newness of it all. You're excited about your shiny new job in this shiny new salon.

That's why it's important to take time after the interview to think about the whole picture: the people, the vibe, the services. You're going to spend more time in this place than with your partner and kids. You're going to be miserable if the culture doesn't match your own brand and values.

Some people go to workshops and come up with a vision statement or core values and plaster them on the website, but they don't really mean anything. They're lip service.

If you see and hear things during an interview that don't match the website, that's a huge red flag. If you're looking for a career—a salon home—where you can grow and contribute, you won't be happy in a place that doesn't hold the same values.

"WHY" CHECK

Go back to your journal and find your "why." Does that still ring true? More importantly, does it seem like this salon will help you fulfill your "why"? Can you see yourself staying there for the long haul, building relationships, and growing in your ability to serve clients?

Let me be the angel on your shoulder, reminding you to look at what you want out of this career. Will this salon allow you to build the life you want? Will you be able to spend time with your kids after school or travel the world? Did you sense a vibe that goes with what you want out of this career?

This industry is such a gift. Yes, you're cutting and coloring hair, but you're doing so much more. It's not about the hair. You have an opportunity to touch people, to change lives.

Reach Out

At the end of the interview, the person should have told you the next steps, specifically, when you can expect to hear from them.

If they said they'll get back to you in a few days, give it a few days and then be proactive. Reach out. Show that you are seriously interested.

You can keep it short and sweet because you've already sent the thank-you email, for example:

Hi, _____.

We discussed that I would hear from you by Friday. I know you are super busy, so I wanted to get this back to the top of your inbox and say once again how much I enjoyed talking with you. If there is anything else you need from me, please don't hesitate to reach out. I would love the opportunity to join your impressive team.

If you don't hear back after a few days, go into your sent folder, find the email, and click Reply. Then add a short note, like, "I just wanted to put this at the top of your inbox" and followed by the original thank you. If you still haven't heard back, it's time to move on to another salon.

RESEARCH, INTERVIEW, REPEAT

If you've done your homework, you are in the driver's seat during the interview. You know what they might ask, and you know how to answer. You also know what you want to ask, and what you're looking for in their answers. Take ownership of the process before, during, and after to put yourself in the best position for success.

Even if you've done all that, you may not get the job. The salon may have interviewed someone who is a better fit, or they may have decided to hold off on hiring for the moment. It could also be that the interviewer realizes that her salon won't be a good fit. She sees that this place won't serve you.

Mirror Mirror is very, very fast-paced. To do well, stylists have to be willing to put themselves out there and go for it. Extremely shy people won't do well here, and it would be unkind of me to hire someone knowing they will struggle. No matter how sweet and nice they are, they won't thrive.

The salon owner might be doing the same for you. She knows things about the salon that you can't know from one informational interview and one job interview. She may realize that you won't grow there for whatever reason. Different flowers thrive in different environments. You have to find the one that's right for you.

Remember what I said early on: my goal is to help you find a salon home. A beautiful long-term marriage, not a temporary date. And marriages aren't one-sided. Both partners have to believe this is the best fit.

If you don't get an offer, that's okay. Keep moving forward. Keep researching and interviewing. Remember my story: I worked at three different salons, thinking each one would be perfect and none of them were. Your second choice may end up being the place for you.

If you do get an offer, congratulations! In the next chapter, we'll talk about evaluating and accepting that offer, as well as starting your new job.

Chapter 11

MAINTAIN THE MOMENTUM

"KATHERINE" BEGAN WORKING AT MIRROR MIRROR AS AN INTERN while she was still in school. She was a star. With some of our senior stylists mentoring her, she started building her clientele, cleaned up her online presence, and did all the things outlined in this book. She supported the stylists and found things to do when she had downtime. We were looking forward to hiring her as an apprentice and beyond.

And then she quit.

In cosmetology school, Katherine was top of her class. At the salon, she went back to the bottom of the totem pole just like everyone else. But Katherine wasn't happy at the bottom. Based on what she had learned in school, she had her own ideas of how things should be done. When things weren't done the way she thought they should be, she took the education she had received and moved on.

Here's the challenge: your schooling and ambition got you the job offer, but now you have to Etch-a-Sketch your brain. You need to forget everything you think you know about doing hair and learn how they do things at this salon.

You researched this salon. You evaluated them during the interview. You took the job. Now you have to trust the process.

Too often, people like Katherine forget the plan they heard during the interview: They work X amount of time as an apprentice. They can start seeing clients after Y number of months. The dress code includes A but not B.

Then they start wondering why it's taking so long to get on the floor. They start pushing the dress code boundary or complaining about the commission structure or scheduling or the commute.

When you start your apprenticeship, you are starting over. You are also beginning two jobs: you're an apprentice, but you are also interviewing to be a stylist. Your new employer wants to see if you are trainable. They want to see that you live up to your résumé and interview. They want to make sure you're the perfect fit they thought you were—both as an apprentice and a future stylist.

You spent a lot of time and energy thinking about your "why," identifying your brand, building a client list, cleaning up your online presence, researching salons, and preparing for the interview.

Don't slow down now!

When you receive that offer (positive thinking!), take time to evaluate it before you say yes. And when you walk in the door on that first day, start treating your new job like the dream job it is. This chapter will show you how.

ACCEPTING THE OFFER

This isn't a corporate industry, so the offer itself may not be a formal letter. It may be as casual as an email saying, "We'd love for you to be our next apprentice!" or "We'd love to have you join our team!"

Either way, congratulations are in order. You did it!

The next step is to evaluate the terms of the offer and make sure you understand exactly what you're agreeing to. Chances are many of the following questions were covered in the interview. Now is the time to get all the nitty-gritty details.

Also, if you're looking at this as a long-term home, you want to know what your career will look like now and at the next stage. Before you sign anything, make sure you fully understand the following as they apply to being an apprentice *and* a stylist. You probably already discussed some of these things in the interview. This is just a reminder to make sure the info in the offer matches what you expected.

- **Compensation:** What is the salary? Do you earn commission? If so, what is the percentage?
- **Education:** Do they offer classes? How often? Are they required? If you come across a class outside the salon, do they contribute to the cost? Can you take time off to take classes?
- **Vacation policy:** What does time off look like? How far in advance do you need to tell them? (Note: if you already know that you need time off for a planned vacation or your sister's wedding, now is the time to say something.)
- **Benefits package:** Do they offer health insurance? How much does it cost? Do they offer a 401(k) plan? Do they match a percentage of your contributions?
- **Dress code:** What is the dress code? Can you wear sneakers? Trucker hats? Don't assume anything.
- **Apprenticeship program:** How long is the program? Is it self-paced? Do you work off a checklist? Can you bring in your own model? Are you shadowing one stylist, or do you rotate?
- **Tools:** Who provides what tools? Do you need your own hair dryer? Curling iron? Round brushes? Salons usually provide shampoo and color, and stylists usually provide their own shears, but just make sure you know what to expect.
- **Schedule and start date:** When is your first day? Will you have a formal orientation? What will your weekly schedule look like? How do you handle lunch breaks? Is there time to go out, or should you bring your own food?

In the days following the interview, create your own list using these questions. That way you're ready if they happen to call and offer you a job. If the salon emails you the offer, then you can respond by asking your questions.

The salon may ask you to sign an agreement to work as a stylist for a year or two after you finish your apprenticeship. Think of it from their perspective: They've just spent a year training you. They want to get something from their investment. They want to make sure you're not going to jump ship when you're done and let another salon benefit from the time and money they've poured into you.

On the other hand, the salon may not have you sign an agreement to work a certain amount of time. We don't at Mirror Mirror because we want people who show up and work hard because they want to—not because they signed some piece of paper.

Before you sign anything, let someone else look at the offer. You could ask your cosmetology school teacher, but I also recommend asking someone outside the industry like a parent or spouse. Vacation time and benefits in particular are handled differently in other industries, so someone who works outside a salon might bring up good questions to ask.

As the final step in evaluating, get everything in writing: the policies related to compensation, education, vacation, benefits, dress code, culture, apprenticeship expectations, tools, start date, and schedule. If you discuss these things on the phone, send a follow-up email recapping the major points and say something like, "I just want to recap our conversation. Here are my takeaways. Please let me know if I missed anything."

Once you know you're all on the same page and you agree to everything being offered, there's only one thing left to do: say yes!

After you accept the offer, the salon should follow up with information about your first day, who you check in with, what to bring, and so on. If they don't, then email a formal acceptance and let them know you're looking forward to getting more specifics. You can keep it really simple: "I'm looking forward to starting on X day at Y time. Who should I ask for when I arrive?"

YOUR FIRST DAY

The day has come!

Approach your first day the same way you did your interview: be early! You absolutely cannot be late on your first day.

You also don't want to come running through the door right on time. You know the route. You know how long it takes to get there. Plan a fifteen-minute buffer at the very least.

Here are a few other guidelines for maintaining the momentum on your first day:

- As you did for the interview, follow the dress code and crank it up about 10 percent.
- Make sure you have all of your tools: shears and whatever else they told you to bring.
- If you already asked about the lunch arrangements, then you'll know what to expect. If you didn't, it's probably best to bring your lunch on the first day and watch what others do.
- If you are given specific tasks, do them. If you run out of things to do, look around. Is there hair to be swept? Are there foils to be torn? The person you're shadowing should give you a general idea of what to do, but you're also expected to hop in where you see a need. Stay busy, especially on that first day. Show people you are there to help and learn.

Most importantly, be open. You've done your due diligence and landed your dream gig, but even with all the research in the world, something unexpected may come up. Just go with it. No place is perfect. *The ambitious stylist stays flexible and absorbs everything she can.*

TWO JOBS NOW

When you start your apprenticeship, you will really have two jobs: being an excellent apprentice to other stylists *and* learning what you need to know for your own future as a stylist. In many ways, it will be like cosmetology school. Your goal is to absorb all the information, ideas, and skills that you can.

APPRENTICE

As an apprentice, your job is to make the stylists' job easier. Their job is to teach you the ins and outs of being a great stylist so you will be prepared when you hit the floor. It's a perfect partnership.

Let's consider your part first: You're there to support. Do you see hair on the floor? Sweep it up. Does a stylist ask you to wash someone's hair? Do it with a smile on your face. Is it three o'clock and no one has eaten? Offer to get food. Is a stylist out of water? Refill her bottle.

Many apprentices are fine with this arrangement at first. Then they start getting antsy. They start asking questions about when they can see clients and get on the floor. Like Katherine, they forget the plan.

This doesn't mean you can never ask questions like these. But hold your tongue during your first day, first week, even your first month. Keep your head down and absorb as much as you can before you start asking anything of your new salon home. Show your ambition in your actions, more than your questions. When you have questions, save them in your phone. There will come a time when you can ask them, but you need to learn the salon's way first.

Your apprenticeship is a marathon. It's hard. Every day your makeup, outfit, and attitude need to be intentional and borderline interview-ready. You will be supporting stylists, learning the salon policies, and honing your skills. You will get to see clients at some point. But you have to be patient.

VOICES FROM THE FIELD

Remember Greg? He landed an apprenticeship at a high-end salon in New York, and then discovered that his job for the first three months was to hand out robes and tea. Then he graduated to shampooing. He could have easily gotten discouraged and said, "I'm outta here!" But he didn't, and his persistence has paid off.

Here's Greg's advice about sticking with your apprenticeship:

I think such an important thing to do when apprenticing (unless there are certain things/conditions you can't change or handle) is stick it out and don't move salons. Do the whole program and get on the floor. The experience of being in the hair industry changes once you are on the floor. I also find the most successful hair stylists are the ones who don't salon hop and stay building at one place.

If you are assigned to one stylist, that person should never have to find you. Be available. If she asks you to shampoo one client or get coffee for another, do it and then come right back. Be a boomerang.

You might feel nervous and shy and be tempted to stay in the break room folding towels because you don't know what else to do. Wrong answer.

If you're not sure what to do first, ask. If the phone rings, and a client needs to be checked out, and another client needs to be shampooed, and towels are backed up, what's the priority? That's a fair question. Ask that early on in your apprenticeship so you know how the salon prioritizes responsibilities.

If you're in the right salon, your relationship with the stylists will be like a marriage: as you take care of them, they will pour back into you to make sure you're getting what you need to learn and grow.

It's not a 50–50 relationship; each side is 100 percent all in. If your focus is "When do *I* get to see clients?" "When is *my* lunch?" "What time do *I* get to go home?" then you're going to have irritated stylists (and leadership) who are less inclined to help.

And you need their help. That's the other side of the apprenticeship coin: learning and growing so you can become a stylist in this salon.

In the midst of serving their own clients, stylists are keeping an eye on you: Do you know how to shampoo correctly? Do you know how to tone? Do you know how to deliver an excellent blowout? (See, I told you that was an important skill!) They will help you become a technically good stylist.

They will also show you how they interact with their guests, pre-book them, offer them take-home products, and all the "not hair" part of this job.

Many people nail the interview—perfect hair, perfect makeup, perfect attitude, perfect answers. Then on day two, they start slipping. They're running late. They don't put on makeup. They wear a hat when hats are specifically forbidden. They start asking for vacation time way too early in the game.

If you want this to be a long-term relationship, you have to maintain the momentum. You have to keep that interview state of mind.

This will be a lot easier if you pick a salon that matches your style. You'll be used to dressing for the role because you already do it every day. If you put on a fake front for the apprenticeship interview, however, you've dug yourself a big hole. If you're trying to be something you're not, you're going to get tired. And as we've said, this year is going to be tiring enough.

A CAUTIONARY TALE

Despite all of your preparation, you may have made the wrong choice. It happens. We've hired people who end up not fitting and we have to let them go. Like "Claire," for example.

During the interview, Claire seemed like she belonged at Mirror Mirror. She had the right style, attitude, and ambition. Her online presence was professional, and her brand was consistent with our own.

Within a week of starting, however, Claire started showing up late—even though we are very clear that punctuality is nonnegotiable. She fell asleep during a meeting. She thought she was above tearing foils. She would also pop into my office every week or so with questions like, "When can I work with _____?" and "When is the next rotation?"—even though the answers to these questions had been clearly spelled out. She even admitted that her intention was to do her apprenticeship and bounce.

About two months after she had been hired, we let Claire go.

The same thing can happen on the other side: the owner may put on a great interview and say all the right things. The website may portray a dream scenario. The stylists may seem to be friendly on the day you visit.

Then a few weeks in, you realize reality is much different. You hear the gossip in the break room. You see the unprofessional and unfriendly interactions. You feel the competition and big egos among the stylists.

It happens. You haven't done anything wrong.

If this is the case, give the job a month to make sure your first impressions are correct, then go back to your list of salons and start pursuing your second (or third) choice. Don't wait four or five months. You'll be deep into an apprenticeship and then have to start over. Better to get out fast. Don't waste your time and energy, or the salon's.

STYLIST

Your apprenticeship is leading to one thing: becoming a stylist. The ultimate goal is to get you on the floor.

As part of your apprenticeship, the salon should have clearly laid out a plan to get there. (You asked that question, right?) At Mirror Mirror, for example, apprentices are 100 percent supporting and learning for the first half of the program. For the second half, they divide their time between supporting stylists and serving clients. Other salons might have a checklist of services: once you complete all the services required for the quantity required, you are finished! Or they might require a certain amount of time: one year apprenticing regardless of skill or effort.

As part of your transition to stylist, the salon needs to see your skills, which means you'll need to find and bring in models to work on. If you've been doing blowouts and offering discounted services while you're in school, you should have no trouble finding a model. You might have some difficulty finding someone willing to chop off their hair and get a pixie, but otherwise, you're offering regular, simple services: blowout, trim, highlight. The model gets a free service; you get to check off a task on your apprentice-to-stylist checklist. Win–win.

The salon knows you've been playing kitchen beautician on your mom, sister, and/or friends. They know you have at least a small clientele. At some point during your apprenticeship, they need to give you time to work on them in the salon. If they don't, that's a red flag—one you would have ideally found out about before you ever took the job.

For a while, the plan for seeing your own clients might look like forty hours as an apprentice, and then seeing your people in the salon after work. That means you might be doing fifty to sixty hours a week for a while, but know that it's only temporary.

As part of a team-based salon, you'll probably be given some clients. Pretend you're not. Clients you find will be "stickier" than those who are given to you. So, keep networking throughout your apprenticeship and beyond. Keep posting on social media. Keep building that client list. Maintain the momentum.

Journal Challenge

Write a letter to your future stylist self, detailing all the goals you have for your career. Tell yourself how you want to travel to X, drive a Y, and/or give back to the community. Then hide the letter in a safe place and set a reminder on your phone to open the letter in a year or two. Hopefully you'll be smiling big because you're living the life you dreamed of.

REFILL THE BALLOON

Maleah is a Color Specialist at Mirror Mirror. During her apprenticeship interview, she asked, "How long does it take to get through the apprenticeship program?"

"Most people finish in ten to twelve months," I replied.

"I'm going to finish faster than anyone."

"Well, I'm excited to see that."

I was skeptical because I had heard that before. Most new apprentices think they'll finish faster than others, but they don't have the stamina to maintain the momentum.

Maleah did. She finished in nine months.

She worked sixty hours a week during the second half of the program because she was fulfilling her apprenticeship duties during the day and then seeing clients at night. She never took time off. Many weeks she was in the salon all seven days.

Then she made it to the floor and took her foot off the gas. She turned in lower numbers than when she was an apprentice, probably because she was exhausted and burned out. She went on vacations and wasn't as proactive about finding new clients even though she now had twice the amount of time behind the chair.

I had a little talk with Maleah and told her it was time to get back on the horse. She did. Now she's been on the floor for less than a year, and she's on pace to hit six figures.

Let Maleah be an example in three ways: (1) she was ambitious; (2) she maintained the momentum for the whole year of her apprenticeship; (3) she put in the hours, built her client list, stayed focused and inquisitive, and made it to the floor faster than most people.

In the process, however, she burned herself out. She took her foot off the gas once she became a stylist. As a result, her numbers dropped. But only briefly, and once she rallied she came back better than ever!

In Chapter 1, I asked you to brainstorm a list of activities to help you cope with the "bad hair days" during cosmetology school. That list can come in handy during your apprenticeship, too, when you will essentially be doing two jobs. Take care of yourself, whether that means having a spa day or walking your dog. Find ways to keep yourself from getting burned out. Your social life may take a hit—that's okay. You are here for the marathon!

Maintaining the momentum is an active choice. The balloon is going to lose a little air day after day. That's only natural. But it's your responsibility to find ways to refill it.

CONCLUSION

RIGHT OUT OF COSMETOLOGY SCHOOL, TESS TOOK A JOB AS AN assistant at a big salon in her hometown. She had been to this salon as a client and loved the vibe: beautiful buildings, luxurious interiors, high-end products, consistent service. She figured working there would provide the same personalized, high-quality experience. Wrong.

As an assistant, Tess wasn't much more than a maid. She swept hair and cleaned shampoo bowls. She expected this kind of work, but she also expected it to be short term. She was hired with the promise of being able to apply to the apprentice program fairly quickly. But three months went by, then six, then nine, and she was still sweeping and cleaning.

Plus, Tess realized the work culture was very different from the customer experience. Even the apprentices weren't treated that well. They spent almost the whole day shampooing rather than practicing techniques and learning how to be a stylist, and they weren't guaranteed a position once they completed their program. Tess had a sinking feeling that she had made the wrong decision in working there.

Finally, she talked to a friend from cosmetology school—a friend who happened to be an apprentice at Mirror Mirror (it really does pay to make friends in school!). Tess liked what she heard. The culture, values, and apprenticeship plan seemed much more aligned with what she wanted, so she decided to apply.

That was nearly three years ago. In that time, Tess has moved from apprentice, to new talent with a crazy schedule, to stylist who only works four days a week, has weekends off, spends time with her friends, and can travel when she wants.

That doesn't mean it was easy. Tess basically had to write off the nine months she spent at the other salon and start at the beginning, but she was willing to do that to ensure she was at the right place. She was paired with an educator who provided guidance as she worked on clients. What a breath of fresh air, considering she never touched a client's hair in her nine months as an assistant.

Tess worked hard as an apprentice and she crushed it. When she moved to the floor, she had a full clientele but the hard work didn't stop. Her schedule was packed that first year, and she didn't have weekends off. Her second year, her numbers increased month after month. She is now on track to be on our Extension Specialty Team and to make six figures. Tess is living her dream life in her dream salon.

Like Tess—and me and many others—you may not find your salon home on the first try. That's completely normal. Just don't quit. Be willing to stop, reassess, and pivot as needed to find the perfect fit. Go back to your research. Do another informational interview. Apply for another job.

Your dream salon is out there. It just may take a few tries to find it.

LET'S REVIEW

Remember our discussion in Chapter 2 about studying and reviewing class material? The same applies to the tips and tricks in this book.

In each chapter, you were asked to think about where you are and where you're headed. For easy reference, I've gathered all of the journal challenges here, along with a quick summary about each chapter's content. Check this section often as you move closer to graduation, and go back to each chapter for the details as needed.

Chapter 1: Start with the End in Mind. Time to dream: What do you want out of this career? Where do you want to work? What kind of stylist do you want to be? Answering these questions up front will help you weather the tough days in school.

Challenges:

- Why did you go to cosmetology school?
- What kind of clients do you want to work with? What service do you want to be known for?
- Look at the bullet list of questions in the What Kind of Salon? section, and write down your answers. Let yourself dream in vivid detail: sights, sounds, smells.

Chapter 2: Classroom Time. While in school, you have one goal: pass the boards and get your license. Figure you out what study skills you need to do that. And while you're in school, use the time to practice some soft skills that will come in handy down the road.

Challenges:

- What type of learner are you—visual, auditory, read/write, or kinesthetic? If you're not sure, do a Google search for "What type of learner are you?" and take a couple of the quizzes. Then do what you need to do to study and learn in the way that works best for you.
- Write down three great things about life today. Make this gratitude practice an everyday thing so you can remember the good things when school is getting you down.

Chapter 3: Networking. Don't wait until you graduate to build a clientele. Start now! Create a List of Twenty as a jumping-off point. Then start inviting people in for free or discounted services. Even if you have ten clients by the time you graduate, you will be ahead of most.

Challenge:

- Using the bullet list of potential people in your life, make a list of the next twenty people you'll reach out to.

Chapter 4: Blowouts Are the Gateway. Blowouts are a low-risk, high-reward way to build trust and fill out your books. Learn how to invite people in and then deliver a top-notch service.

Challenge:

- Who will you invite to come in for a blowout? Use your journal to brainstorm ten people you can bring in.

Chapter 5: Personal Brand. Whether you realize it or not, you have a brand. It comes across in your words, actions, hair, makeup, clothing, and more. Ambitious stylists decide what brand they want to put out there and take intentional steps to create it.

Challenges:

- What is your personal brand? In other words, how do people see you based on your words, actions, and appearance?
- Is that how you want to be seen, specifically as a stylist? If not, how do you want to be seen?
- For each of the items in this checklist, ask yourself: (1) What is my brand in this area? (2) Is that the brand I want? (3) If not, what changes can I make?
    - My stylist superpower
    - My clothing style
    - My hairstyle
    - My makeup style
    - My personality strength

Chapter 6: Online Presence. Online presence is a big part of your personal brand. Learn from the examples of "Abby," "Madison," and "Chloe." Use social media to let future employers and clients get to know you, like you, and trust you.

Challenge:

- What do you need to do after reading this chapter? Write out your commitment in your journal.

Chapter 7: Salon Search. Don't scroll during class. Start researching your dream salon right now! Take a look at their websites, check out their brand, and consider their size and location. If you want to start off in an independent, booth rental model, this chapter (and the rest of the book) won't apply to you right now. Feel free to come back anytime!

Challenge:

- Find your dream salon!
  - Google "Best salon in _____ [your city]."
  - Ask your favorite teacher what salon they picture you in.
  - Use social media hashtags to search for stylists and salons in your area.
  - Look at the three lists and see if any names pop up on all three.

Chapter 8: Informational Interviews. Informational interviews are the tool you didn't know you needed! Use them to gain information about the salon culture, work environment, and owner and to put yourself top of mind if you later apply for a job. Still intimidated by an informational interview? Book a blowout at your dream salon(s).

Challenge:

- After each interview, do a gut check: How did you feel when you walked in? How about when you left?

Chapter 9: Résumé Building. In our industry, résumés are less formal—more like a one-page snapshot that shows the salon who you are and what you can do. Remember to include a photo, as well as the work experience, certifications, and skills that show you are a perfect fit.

Challenge:

- Make a list of the résumé sections mentioned in the chapter. Then brainstorm what you could say in each section and evaluate: (1) which sections need some work and (2) which sections need to be pared down.

Chapter 10: The Interview. Don't wait until you graduate to start getting ready for your job interview. Spread out your preparation using the timeline in this chapter so you'll be calm and confident when the day arrives. And don't forget to follow up!

Challenge:

- To help you reflect, pull out your journal and answer the following questions:
  - What do you think went well?
  - Did you stumble over a certain question? How would you answer it next time?
  - Is there a question you wish you would have asked?
  - What did you like about the salon environment? What did you dislike?
  - Did you have a "goosebumps moment"?
  - Did you at any point want to run for the hills? Did a comment or observation make you question whether the salon is the place for you?
  - Can you see yourself working there?

Chapter 11: Maintain the Momentum. You got a job offer. Congratulations! Now take time to evaluate the terms before you accept.

And from day one, keep your foot on the gas. You're not only working as an apprentice. You're interviewing for your dream job as a stylist.

Challenge:

- Write a letter to your future stylist self, detailing all the goals you have for your career. Then put it in a safe place and put a reminder on your phone to open it in a year or two.

Journal Challenge

Here's your final challenge: don't quit.

Don't stop.

Don't take your foot off the gas.

Nothing will unwind everything we've talked about so far more than thinking you've arrived. Top stylists who have been in the industry for twenty-plus years still spend time on refining their skills, tracking their numbers, and asking for referrals. They may not spend as much time on networking or social media, but they still do it.

Because school is hard and building a successful career takes work, you need a reason to keep going. Your final challenge is to complete this thought in your journal:

I won't quit because _____.

You can even take it a step further and email me (MLK@theambitiousstylist.com). In the subject line, write, "I won't quit," and then tell me your reason in the email. You will encourage me at the same time you challenge yourself.

BEYOND THE BLIP

Remember the book's opening story? I told my roommate, boss, and mom that I was quitting my high-paying job and going to cosmetology school. It's now fifteen years later. How did that decision work out for everyone involved?

Well, the roommate ended up being the ultimate model during those early years. She let me try all sorts of hairstyles and techniques, though she probably didn't love the outcome every time. The boss is one of our best clients at Mirror Mirror and is still cheering me on. And my mom is not only my biggest cheerleader; she also plays a pivotal role as Mirror Mirror's Queen of Culture and Team Cheerleader, helping me celebrate every birthday and anniversary for our growing team of nearly fifty people.

Fifteen years ago, losing my cute apartment, nice car, and fancy heels was quite traumatic. Though I love my mom, moving back in with her at twenty-seven was not ideal. But now that's all in the rearview mirror. Because I took a chance, followed my dreams, and worked very hard, I now have all of the things I gave up and more. I have grown a family while building the career and lifestyle I wanted, and get to wear what I want to work every day.

Even an optimist like me has to admit cosmetology school was hard. But now I see it was a short but necessary blip on the road to greater things. I married a guy I met during cosmetology school, and one of my cosmetology school besties stood next to me on our wedding day. The owner of my school recently attended the grand opening of Mirror Mirror's new location, and we still text each other frequently. I may not have had my own apprenticeship as a new stylist, but I've had the honor of training and mentoring many, many apprentices along the way.

My hope is that you gain the same perspective about your time in school. Yes, it may be uninspiring or tedious at times. But in the scheme of things, those months are so brief. Plus you've just gained eleven chapters of things you can do to make the most of that time. I hope you use this book until it becomes dog-eared and tattered.

Look back at the checklists and action items. Review the reality checks and journal challenges. Be an ambitious stylist before you ever stand behind a chair. You can do this!

ACKNOWLEDGMENTS

MOST OF ALL I WANT TO THANK GOD, WHO HAS GRANTED ME countless blessings, knowledge, and the privilege to bring this book to life (Philippians 4:13).

To Trevor, my partner in all adventures. I share this book and all of my successes with you. Thank you for being my constant calm and for pushing me to my fullest potential. You are the best thing that ever happened to me!

To Mom, my cheerleader and role model. This book is a tribute to you. Thank you for leading by example and showing me what ambition is. Thank you for believing in me, for cheering me on from the sidelines, and for always being my biggest fan.

To Ford and Luke, my precious boys, who remind me every day of the boundless joy and wonder that life has to offer. May your adventures be wild, your hearts be brave, and your spirits always soar. I hope this book is a constant reminder to find your purpose and pursue it with everything you've got!

To Jeff, thank you for pushing me into the world of entrepreneurship. Thank you for teaching me about all of life's opportunities that are afforded to me each day—even when I just wanted to sleep in!

To Gilbert, thank you for the countless hours of dedication in the trenches of the early years of Mirror Mirror. We would not be where we are today without your unwavering dedication and support. Finding a friend and partner in business is a rarity, and I found both in you. Your fingerprints will always be ingrained in the foundation of Mirror Mirror.

To Bryon, the yin to my yang. Thank you for being my tether and for keeping us grounded and steadfast in our mission! Your dedication to me and the entire Mirror Mirror team is inspiring and a testament to the leader you are.

To Carolyn, thank you for taking a big leap with me and Mirror Mirror. Thank you for leading by example and, most importantly, for your friendship. We have taken "doing life together" to the next level, and I wouldn't have it any other way.

To Brynn, thank you for your friendship and for trusting me with so many ebbs and flows of your career. Thank you for not hanging up your apron when you moved to Texas and for teaching us all so much. Watching you grow and lead has been a joy, and I can't wait to see where we go next.

To Midge, the OG. Thank you for sticking around through all of our growing pains and keeping us laughing along the way! We have both grown so much together!

To Brett W., thank you for your friendship, laughs, and support from the old days of previous salon traumas to the present-day of fun at Mirror Mirror.

To Dani, the Skipper to my Barbie. Thank you for the many hours you sat in my chair letting me "play hair" and for always being the perfect model and sidekick.

To Antony, thank you for helping me GROW. Your mentorship and guidance have kept us on track and you have been a large part of the many stages of our growth.

Randy and Wendi, thank you for your dedication to cosmetology students. Your genuine passion for seeing all students succeed is a rarity in this industry. Thank you for planting the early seeds in me for what it would take to be my best!

To Heather, my dance partner. Thank you for being the first person to cheer me on in my cosmetology journey.

To Amy, from the best boss to the best client. Thank you!

To Alli, thank you for being the brightest light in cosmetology school. You made a tough time tolerable and your friendship kept me going.

To Anna, Mandee, Rachelle, and Meghan, thank you for being my childhood guinea pigs. My recess clients. The slumber parties, dances, home videos, and early creativity continue to feed me and make me smile.

To Rob, thank you for your creative eye in the branding evolution of Mirror Mirror and for many laughs along the way. There's no one I would rather write a fake jingle with!

To Andrew, thank you for being a sounding board on many of the creative decisions of this book.

To Alyssa, thank you for keeping my head on straight and keeping me accountable. Your listening ear has been a great sense of peace throughout this entire process.

To Brandy, Brett, Payton, Irene, Lindsey, Aili, Nataly, and Amy, thank you for being generous in sharing your "why." I appreciate your honesty and transparency and know so many students will be encouraged when they see themselves in you.

To Greg Pike, Anthony Holguin, Chris Jones, Melanie Hasson, Taylor Dellatorre, Sarah Cabral, Stephanie Brown, Chelle Neff, Clint Torres, Evan McDonald, Alex McDonald, Tess Reuter, and Maleah Ramos, thank you for sharing your "voice from the field" to the next generation of hairdressers. I know your tips and advice will be wildly beneficial to them as they start their careers!

To Nataly, Connor, Maleah, Tess, Payton, Connor, Lisa, Brandy, Lily G, and every previous apprentice who has ever worked at Mirror Mirror. Thank you for trusting me to help you launch your career and for trusting the process. To those of you who are still around, it is my greatest joy to watch you grow and succeed.

Thank you to Liv, Emma, Carlie, Haven, and Madison, our existing apprentices throughout the writing of this book. You have been an incredible sounding board and voice of cosmetology students everywhere. As Mrs. George from *Mean Girls* would say, "Oh, you girls keep me young!"

Thank you to Gail and the entire Scribe team for helping me find my voice.

And last but certainly not least, thank you to my entire Mirror Mirror Family. You can't be a home base for *The Ambitious Stylist* without unwavering ambition. You are the team I dreamed about. Pinch me.

ABOUT THE AUTHOR

MARTHA LYNN KALE began her career in advertising before following her lifelong passion for beauty and enrolling in cosmetology school. Just three years after graduation and after gaining experience at three very different salons, Martha Lynn founded Mirror Mirror, a salon known for helping clients love what they see. Mirror Mirror has been included on the Inc. 5000 list of the fastest-growing private companies in America three times, as well as the Salon Today 200 by *Salon Today* magazine for the past eight years. Martha Lynn lives in Austin, Texas, with her husband and two sons.

Printed in the USA
CPSIA information can be obtained
at www.ICGtesting.com
LVHW042343230824
789028LV00004B/18